Changing Local Government

CPMR Research Report
5

Changing Local Government
A Review of the Local Government Modernisation Programme

Richard Boyle
Peter C. Humphreys
Orla O'Donnell
Joanna O'Riordan
Virpi Timonen

First published in 2003
by the
Institute of Public Administration
57-61 Lansdowne Road
Dublin 4
Ireland
in association with
The Committee for Public Management Research

www.ipa.ie

British Library Cataloguing in Publication Data
A catalogue record for this book is available from the British Library.

ISBN 1 902448 98 7
ISSN 1393-9424

Cover design by Butler Claffey, Dún Laoghaire
Typeset by the Institute of Public Administration
Printed by Future Print, Dublin

CONTENTS

Executive Summary

Introduction

This study provides an overview of progress on the implementation of the local government modernisation programme as set out in *Better Local Government – A Programme for Change* (1996). The study focuses on the thirty-four county and city authorities in the Republic of Ireland. Three key questions are addressed: what was intended to be achieved by the modernisation programme; what is happening in practice; and what are the key issues emerging? Evidence for the study findings was obtained from a review of documentation, a series of key informant interviews at both local and central government levels, and a questionnaire survey of county/city managers.

The framework for the study is set out in Figure E1. Three main desired outcomes of the local government modernisation programme are identified: an enhanced community leadership role for local government; the provision of services in a more efficient and effective manner; and the delivery of high-quality services to the users of local authority services. The local government modernisation programme is made up of a number of elements that contribute to each of these outcomes. Each of these elements is investigated in some detail in the study.

Community leadership – an enhanced role for local government

Two significant aims of the local government modernisation programme are to develop political decision making and to widen the role of local government. The intention is to enhance the policy-making role of elected members and to give local government a more prominent role in local development. These twin aims focus on developing the community leadership role of local government.

Developing political decision making: main findings

Strategic policy committees

Strategic policy committees (SPCs) have been established in all county and city councils. The purpose of SPCs is to strengthen the policy-making role of elected councillors and

Figure E.1 Main elements and outcomes of the local government modernisation programme

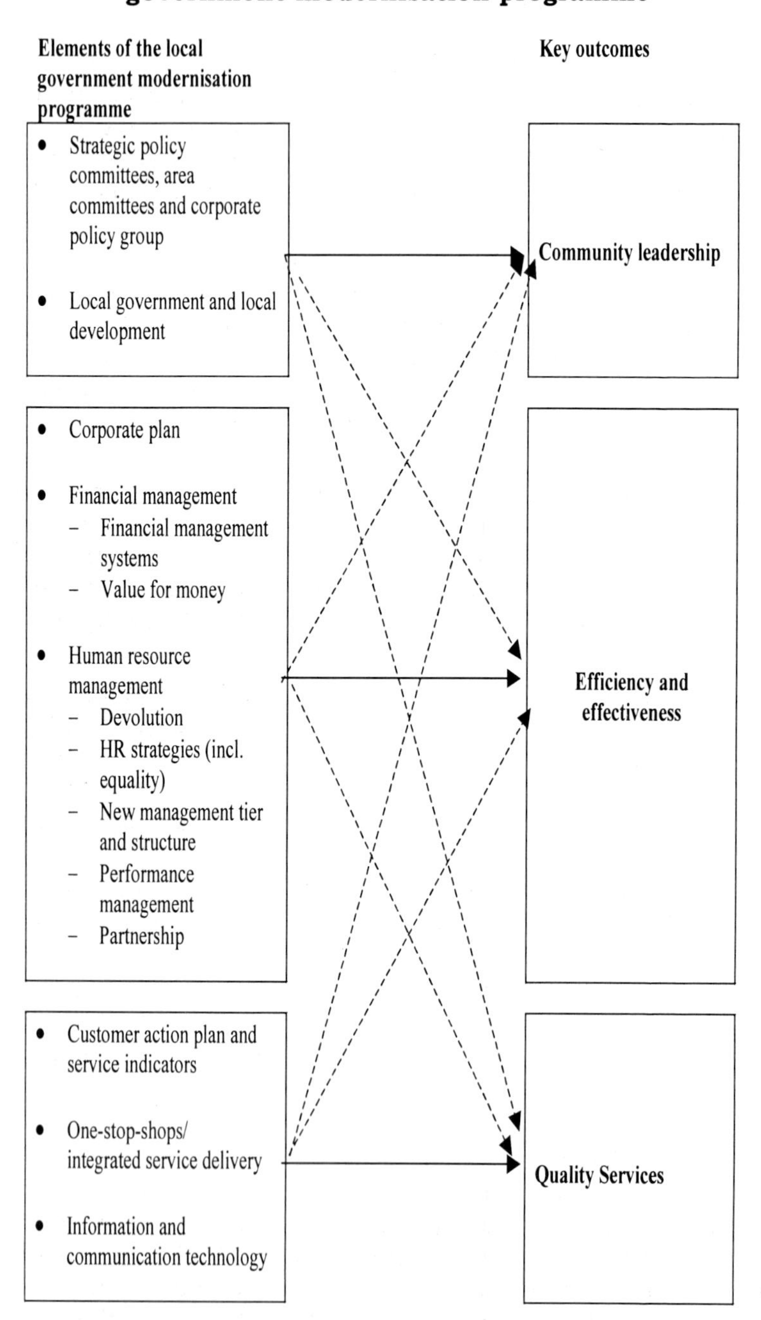

to broaden participation in local government through the direct involvement of sectoral interests.

The effectiveness of SPCs varies significantly across and within authorities, as does the level of participation. Some SPCs are seen to be working well. In others, there is a perceived danger of SPCs turning into 'talking shops' with little relevance to the work of local authorities. This study identifies a number of critical factors which need to be addressed if SPCs are to operate effectively:

- The role of the chair of the SPC. The chair has a vital role in setting the tone for the operation of the SPC. The chairperson should engage with the substantive content issues, facilitate interaction between councillors and sectoral interests and establish links with the full council.
- The supply of meaningful policy issues. Here, the role of council staff, particularly directors of service, in ensuring relevant papers/background material is crucial. The development of research capability within the local authority to enable policy issues to be explored is an important factor.
- The engagement of councillors. The frequency and timing of meetings is important, given the large number of meetings councillors are asked to attend. So too is ensuring that councillors can see the linkage between policy discussions and the delivery of services to their constituents.
- The engagement and legitimacy of sectoral representatives. The process of appointment of sectoral representatives should aim to ensure that they are as representative as practicable. There should be regular feedback between the sector and the representative. Educating representatives on the role and working of local government is also important.

Area committees

Area committees, which focus on council business within designated local authority areas, have been established in the majority of county and city councils. While not needed in all local authorities, where they are in operation they are seen as making a very positive contribution and to be working well. Area committees have enabled local issues to be dealt with at the local level, leaving more time at full council to address council-wide and corporate issues. In the medium to longer-term, the continuing success of area committees in many authorities is likely to be tied in with the extent to which service provision is decentralised to area level and the consequent interaction between area committees and area offices and officials.

Corporate policy groups

The corporate policy group (CPG), comprising the chairpersons of the SPCs, is intended to co-ordinate the work of the various SPCs. The CPG has only had a limited impact in many local authorities to date. Where the CPG is working well, it is seen to (a) act as a useful sounding board to discuss contentious issues before they appear at full council, and (b) enable participating members to be better informed on policy issues. But in many councils the CPG is not seen as giving direction to council priorities. Key determinants of the success or otherwise of the CPG are the openness of the manager and members to working together, and how effectively participating members feed back information to their own parties about the discussions at CPG meetings.

Conclusions

In general, changes in political decision making are about enabling elected members to have more influence in shaping and directing policy. Area committees are widely seen to be working well. The picture with regard to SPCs and the CPG is more patchy. Further work is needed to secure an effective longer-term role for SPCs and the CPG in local authorities.

Widening the role of local government: main findings

In the mid to late 1990s the government recognised the absence of co-ordination among the various centrally determined local development initiatives established during the 1980s and early 1990s, such as LEADER groups, partnership companies and county and city enterprise boards. Government policy was to promote the local authority as the primary co-ordinator of local development activities.

The establishment and operation of county and city development boards (CDBs) has been the major feature in expanding the role of local government in local development and social inclusion. By the end of 2002, all CDBs had published their strategies for economic, social and cultural development. The operation of the CDBs has been greatly facilitated by the creation of the post of director of community and enterprise and associated support staff. Local government is now widely seen as having a stronger role in influencing and co-ordinating local development initiatives.

The building blocks have been put in place to develop collaborative arrangements between local authorities and other public service providers so as to enhance local development. In moving forward, local authorities will need to:

- Develop their research capability. There is need to enhance the evidence base for the implementation of social, economic and cultural strategies. This requires action both within local authorities and in terms of collaboration with other agencies, such as third-level institutions and the Local Government Management Services Board.
- Establish themselves as local leaders in the assessment of needs, policy direction and delivery of public services. Local authorities with their democratic mandate, are well placed to develop a strategic local governance role in terms of local development. The next steps involve a move to shared decision making, shared resources and shared risk taking.

But the ultimate success of local government taking a lead role in local development is not dependent on local authorities alone. Central government departments and their agencies must be given the direction to act in a way that facilitates rather than restricts the local leadership role of local authorities.

Improving the efficiency and effectiveness of services

A significant part of the local government modernisation

programme aims to ensure that the services run by local authorities are run efficiently and effectively. This encompasses planning for service provision and the use of resources, both human and financial.

Planning for service provision: main findings

Local authorities are required to produce corporate plans outlining their main objectives and strategies. The corporate planning process is still relatively new in local government. However, early indications are that managers within local authorities see corporate plans as a useful development. The plans are seen to help give more of a focus on results and greater clarity and consensus on the main objectives to be achieved. The study identifies a number of actions that can be taken to build on this early positive impression and improve the planning process in the future:

- Objectives and strategies should be more clearly defined and specified, and focused on the outcomes to be achieved where possible.
- Citizen/customer expectations and needs, as assessed by customer surveys, panels etc, should be used to identify strategic issues to be addressed.
- It will be important to match resources within the authority to the strategic priorities identified, ensuring that the capacity exists to match the aspirations outlined.
- In ensuring effective implementation and monitoring, there is a need to further develop operational plans and performance indicators within the authority. Practice in the selection and application of indicators should be reviewed so that the information needed to manage more effectively is provided.
- The annual report of the authority should be used to report on progress regarding implementation of the objectives and strategies set out in the corporate plan.

Managing financial resources: main findings

A new computerised financial management system (FMS) has been introduced in local authorities. Significant progress has been made in getting the FMS up and running. The process used to implement the financial management changes has worked well. However, introducing the FMS was a lot more resource-intensive than originally envisaged, and the system less user-friendly than was anticipated. But there is a significant degree of senior management engagement with the FMS. At the same time, there has been an upgrading of the finance function in local authorities, with the creation of head of finance posts and financial/management accountant posts.

Now that the FMS has been introduced in local authorities, the main challenges and benefits associated with the full implementation of the FMS lie ahead. Two particular challenges to be addressed are identified in this study if financial management practice is to be significantly improved:

- There is a cultural change for many managers and staff in moving to a more active engagement with the budgeting process. Designating budget holders and getting them to manage their budgets in a pro-active manner will require significant developments of capability.
- There is a need to introduce better procedures for the costing of service provision and assessment of alternative approaches to service delivery. The financial data now being generated should be used to help in the exploration of alternative delivery mechanisms, including outsourcing, and in the benchmarking of the performance of functions.

Managing human resources: main findings

Human resource management (HRM) was identified as a critical area for reform in the local government modernisation programme. In particular, the introduction of a new management structure with responsibility and accountability for developing strategic thinking was identified as a vital element in supporting the overall change programme.

Some delays were experienced in introducing the new staffing structure, due to industrial relations difficulties and consequent union/management negotiations. By 2002, however, the new management tier of directors of service was in place, and consequent changes in staffing at middle management and other levels either in place or in the process of being introduced. One interesting feature is that local authorities are structuring service and reporting arrangements to directors of service in different ways. It is important that steps are taken to learn from this diverse experience. While one model for all is inappropriate, it could be helpful if good practice and problems associated with different arrangements are identified and lessons learned from this experience. This is an issue that should be followed up by the Local Government Management Services Board.

More generally with regard to HRM reform, a number of issues emerge from this study as needing attention in the future:

- Strategies in relation to the implementation of the HRM agenda should be detailed in the next iteration of corporate plans.
- There is a need for further development of managerial skills and competencies, particularly in the case of middle management and newly promoted staff.
- Outdoor staff need to be more involved in the change programme.
- There is a need to both further develop the strategic HR role of HR units and to increase the role of line managers in the active management of HR issues within their spheres of responsibility.
- The development of a system of performance management and the continuing implementation of training and development programmes are important in helping bed down the new staffing structures.

It is also important to refer to the role of partnership in local authorities in a HR context. Where it has worked well, partnership has led to improved consultation and enhanced opportunities for staff to participate in decision making. In moving forward, if partnership is to develop further, it is important to set clear goals for the process and to engage with more of the harder-edged HR/management issues.

Delivering and securing quality services

This strand of the modernisation programme focuses on identifying and better serving the needs of customers, clients and citizens. Central to this drive for better quality services has been the development of customer action plans, service indicators, more integrated service delivery including one-stop-shops, and the use of information and communications technologies to support and underpin service initiatives.

Customer action plans and service indicators: main findings

Customer action plans

Local authorities are required to produce and publish customer action plans (CAPs) setting out (a) the actions authorities will take to achieve improvements in the quality of public services they are responsible for and (b) how full effect will be given to the public-service wide guiding principles for the delivery of quality customer service.

Overall, CAPs are contributing to planned improvements in areas such as information provision, the specification of service standards and indicators and complaint/appeal handling systems. However, this study identifies a number of actions that can be taken in order to improve the future contribution of CAPs to enhanced customer service:

- Further efforts are needed in many local authorities to drive forward quality improvements in line with the nationally agreed principles for quality customer service.
- There is a need for more widespread adoption of practices such as surveys of the customer base and the use of innovative consultation mechanisms. Systematic follow-on procedures should also be developed to ensure that such survey and consultation exercises are acted upon.
- Improved usage of central level guidance and support, combined with healthy inter-authority competition, co-operation and peer review, should help in improving both the quality and content of CAPs.
- Engagement with external quality frameworks, such as the EU-wide Common Assessment Framework (CAF) can provide a valuable diagnostic tool, help promote joined-up, quality-focused thinking, and provide the opportunity for constructive benchmarking.

Service indicators
Local authorities are required to develop and use performance indicators to measure progress in relation to service standards. The development of these service indicators is at an early stage. There is a need now to review experience to date, identify the degree to which service indicators are being found useful in practice, and explore whether indicators should be developed or changed in the light of experience. In particular, there is scope for more use to be made of comparative benchmarking of performance by authorities, either over time, against standards or with selected groupings of other authorities. More active engagement with local citizens in the development and use of indicators should also be encouraged.

Integrated service delivery and one-stop-shops: main findings
The delivery of more integrated services at local level, with one-stop-shops as a key delivery mechanism for such integration, is a principal component of the move to enhance the quality of service delivery. The intention is that instead of service being organised around bureaucratic structures, they are delivered according to the needs of service users.

In practice, the scale of ambition regarding integrated service delivery varies considerably between local authorities, as does the amount of progress made to date. The more ambitious authorities are striving towards integrating processing of requests and applications, by engaging with different departments and agencies on behalf of individual clients. In terms of moving the integrated service delivery agenda forward, two particular challenges are highlighted by the study:

- Because of the interdependence between the Public Services Broker concept, being developed centrally, and local service delivery units such as integrated service centres, it will be critical to future developments that the links between central and local government are reinforced through greater collaboration and co-ordination.
- Getting different service providers to co-operate can

pose difficulties in practice. Co-location of services is not necessarily the solution in all circumstances; more fundamental is the need to change practices so that service providers integrate and co-ordinate their services in a manner which suits the needs of the service recipient.

Using information and communication technologies: main findings

Increasing the use of information and communication technologies (ICTs) is a significant part of the local government modernisation programme. The aim is to improve the quality of service delivery and decision-making processes. In this context, many local authorities have developed Intranets and Extranets and improved their Internet sites. However, there are still relatively few web-based applications that enable citizens to deal electronically with local authorities. Managers are also concerned about the need to ensure e-inclusion for all citizens.

However, an important point emerging from the study is that the building up of technical capacity on its own does not necessarily mean that work processes or service delivery are fully co-ordinated and integrated. The effective us of ICTs often involves complex organisational changes that do not automatically follow the insertion of technology into local authorities. This view is not necessarily shared by all managers within local authorities at present, and work needs to be done to develop a shared understanding of the organisational changes needed to facilitate achievement of the full benefits of ICTs.

Local government modernisation: an overview

Looking at the actions that have been taken, significant progress has been made in implementing the local government modernisation programme. But the steps taken to date should be seen as the first steps needed to create a vibrant local government service in Ireland. The foundations for progress have now been laid in areas such as financial management, human resource management, service quality and corporate planning. What is needed next is to consolidate and build on those foundations so as to deliver improved services to the public at local level. In moving forward, it is worth noting some of the main challenges to be faced.

When asked about challenges to be addressed in rolling the modernisation programme forward, county and city managers were in no doubt that securing the necessary financial and other resources needed to see implementation through was the main challenge. While recognising the limitations on public finances and the need to determine strategic priorities, there was seen to be a need for continuing support for the modernisation programme to secure full implementation.

The more active involvement of several key groups in moving the modernisation agenda forward has emerged from this study as a challenge. Many elected members, sectoral interest representatives on SPCs, and outdoor staff in local authorities, have only had limited engagement with the change process to date. There is a need for these groups to be more actively associated with change as things move forward.

The leadership and co-ordination role of local government in securing improved public services at local level – the local governance agenda – poses particular challenges. One of the main issues to be addressed here is ensuring 'buy-in' to the leadership role of local authorities by central government departments and agencies. Departments and agencies other than the Department of the Environment and Local Government need to be encouraged to work with and through local authorities on local policy and implementation issues they are engaged in.

Also, in this study a notable feature of the change process which we observed has been the diverse experience that exists across local authorities. Pockets of good practice exist in different authorities, with some moving forward faster than others in some areas. But local authorities are not particularly good at sharing and learning from this diverse experience in a structured way. More effort is needed to encourage and facilitate learning across local authorities.

Finally, there is the continuing challenge of ensuring appropriate supports to enable change. In this study, several examples of support structures which have been put in place and which have facilitated implementation of elements of the modernisation programme have been identified. This is the case particularly with regard to local government and local development, where the national task force, directors of community and enterprise and the Combat Poverty Agency anti-poverty learning network were noted as important structural supports in promoting modernisation.

A key point to emerge from this study is that the place of local government in public administration in Ireland is determined not only by the functions allocated to it or those services local government delivers directly. Equally important is the leadership role played by local government in the overall provision of local public services. To view local authorities as providers of a limited range of services is to miss the point. The potential for local government to influence and shape economic and social development locally is extremely significant. The degree to which this potential is translated into actual benefits will be determined by how local and central government continue to take forward the modernisation agenda.

PART 1

Setting the Scene for the Study

1

Introduction and Background

1 Introduction

1.1 Focus of report

This study provides an overview of progress on the implementation of the local government modernisation programme as set out in *Better Local Government – A Programme for Change* (1996). The study presents a snapshot of progress at one point in time. It also focuses on the champions of change and the dissemination of best practice, with a view to highlighting and promoting good practice. The study covers all of the thirty-four county and city authorities.

1.2 Study background and terms of reference

The terms of reference agreed for this study are that it would:

a) map out the main elements of the local government modernisation programme
b) review progress to date with regard to the implementation of the modernisation programme
c) where appropriate, place local government modernisation in an international context, by examining relevant local government reform initiatives in other jurisdictions
d) draw conclusions as to the impact to date of the local government modernisation programme on local authorities, and indicate future directions of change in the light of national and international experience and best practice.

Figure 1.1 outlines the broad framework for the study. Starting at the national level, there is the overall policy driving the local government modernisation programme.

Figure 1.1 Framework for the local government modernisation study

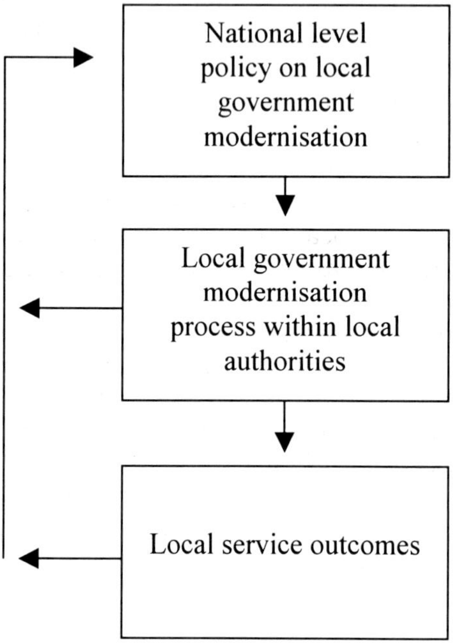

National level policy on local government modernisation

Local government modernisation process within local authorities

Local service outcomes

The main policy documents setting the parameters of the local government modernisation programme are *Better Local Government* (1996), *Modernising Government* (2000) and the *Programme for Prosperity and Fairness* (2000). This policy is informed by a variety of sources. These include:

- Central government departments, particularly the Department of the Environment and Local Government (DELG), with direct responsibility for local government, and the Department of the Taoiseach and Department of Finance, as promoters of the public service modernisation programme. Also the Office of the Ombudsman.
- Local government, trade and professional organisations, such as the County and City Managers Association, the

Local Government Management Services Board and the trade unions.

- State-sponsored bodies with links with local government, such as the Local Government Computer Services Board, the National Roads Authority, and the Environmental Protection Agency.
- International developments in local government modernisation.

The national level policy-making process drives the implementation of the local government modernisation programme within local authorities. The modernisation programme, in turn, aims to deliver improved local service outcomes.

The main elements of the local government modernisation programme and the key outcomes which modernisation aims to bring about are set out in Figure 1.2. These elements and outcomes are derived from *Better Local Government* (1996), *Modernising Government* (2000) and the *Programme for Prosperity and Fairness* (2000). The elements of the modernisation programme form the core units of analysis for this study

Key outcomes

a Community leadership

This outcome focuses on developing an enhanced community leadership role for local government. *Better Local Government* includes chapters on enhancing democracy and on a wider role for local government. *Modernising Government* talks about developing the role of local government in community leadership. The *Programme for Prosperity and Fairness* talks about strengthening and re-invigorating local government to be at the centre of the provision of a wide range of services to the community. The main elements of the modernisation programme related to this outcome are:

- The establishment and operation of strategic policy committees (SPCs) to enhance the corporate role of councillors and encourage community participation and

Figure 1.2 Main elements and outcomes of the local government modernisation programme

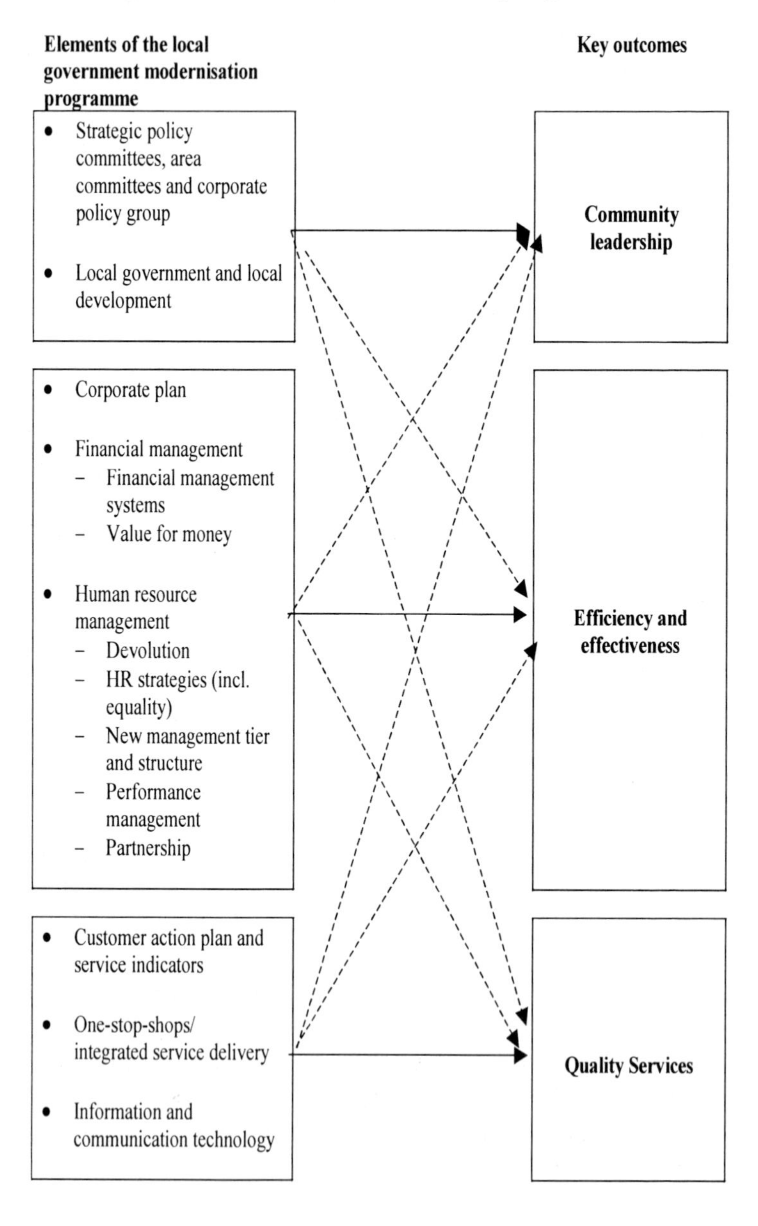

partnership. Each council will have a corporate policy group (CPG) to link the work of its SPCs. These moves are accompanied by the decentralisation of services and decision making at the local level.

- Linking local government and local development, in particular through the county/city development boards, including linkages with voluntary and community organisations. Local development is also concerned with the devolution of appropriate functions from national level to local government.

b Efficiency and effectiveness

This outcome focuses on ensuring that the services run by local authorities are provided in an efficient and effective manner. In chapters on finance and human resources, *Better Local Government* indicates the need to ensure that money is well spent and that staff are properly managed, motivated, involved and trained to deliver cost-effective services. *Modernising Government* highlights the fact that local government renewal aims to significantly improve management and decision-making structures and financial and human resource management. The *Programme for Prosperity and Fairness* talks about strengthening management and staffing structures, providing higher levels of staff development and training, and eliminating obstacles to flexibility and efficiency. The main elements of the modernisation programme related to this outcome are:

- The production of corporate plans to provide the overall framework for the policy and decision-making processes. These plans are to be supplemented by annual operational plans and reviewed annually by the council.
- Changes in financial management practices, in particular
  - the introduction of accrual-based accounting and related new financial management systems;
  - a greater emphasis on value for money, including the audit system.

- Developments in human resource management, including:
  - devolution of HR functions from the DELG to local authorities;
  - the development of HR strategies and initiatives in areas such as recruitment and retention, equality and training and development;
  - the introduction of new management structures, including the creation of a corps of directors to lead each of the main services and to support the SPCs (and allied with the abolition of the dual structure);
  - the introduction of a performance management system;
  - the development of partnership structures to drive the change programme.

c *Quality services*

This outcome focuses on identifying the needs of the customer and the delivery of high-quality services to meet those needs. *Delivering Better Government* has a chapter on quality services, and serving the customer better is one of the core principles of the programme. *Modernising Government* talks of developing the customer service ethos. The *Programme for Prosperity and Fairness* highlights the need to bring services close to the customer and re-emphasises the principle of customer service. The main elements of the modernisation programme related to this outcome are:

- The development of customer action plans, to be incorporated in the corporate plans. These plans, based on consultation, are intended to set standards of service. The plans are to work in conjunction with the application of common service indicators, which are to be reported on in the council's annual report.
- The introduction of one-stop-shops and local area offices, associated with the decentralisation of services.
- The use of information and communication technologies to underpin service delivery initiatives.

1.3 Study approach and methodology

For each of the elements of the local government modernisation programme, a common set of questions was used to guide the approach to data gathering and the presentation of findings. These questions are:

- What was intended to be achieved by the element of the modernisation programme?
- What is happening in practice?
- What are the key issues emerging (this may include an international comparative context) and where to next?

A range of methodological approaches were used to provide the information for this study:

- literature review of national and international developments
- a series of key informant interviews with national level stakeholders (see Appendix 1 for details)
- interviews in a range of local authorities with senior managers involved in implementation of elements of the modernisation programme (see Appendix 1 for details)
- a questionnaire survey (filled in by the county/city manager) sent out to all thirty-four city and county councils (see Appendices 2 and 3 for copies of the questionnaire and replies respectively).

The study commenced in December 2001 and field-work was completed towards the end of 2002.

1.4 Report structure

The study is divided into five parts, each of which has a chapter or chapters associated with it.

Part 1 sets the scene for the study. It includes this introductory chapter and Chapter 2, which provides a brief historical and comparative sketch of local government in Ireland.

Parts 2, 3 and 4 are where the main elements of the modernisation programme are reviewed.

Part 2 addresses the issue of community leadership. Chapter 3 examines the workings of strategic policy committees, area committees and corporate policy groups.

Chapter 4 explores the developing linkage between local government and local development.

Part 3 addresses the issue of efficiency and effectiveness. Chapter 5 examines the corporate plans produced by local authorities, and their usefulness. Chapter 6 looks at financial management developments. Chapter 7 investigates the human resource management changes that have taken place as a result of the modernisation programme.

Part 4 addresses the issue of the delivery of quality services. Chapter 8 reviews the customer action plans and service indicators produced by local authorities. Chapter 9 explores the development of one-stop-shops/integrated service delivery mechanisms as a means of providing better service. Chapter 10 looks at how information and communication technologies are being used to develop services.

Part 5 of the study summarises the main findings. Chapter 11 provides conclusions and recommendations, looking at the local government modernisation programme as a whole.

2

Putting Local Government in Context: a Brief Historical and Comparative Sketch

2.1 Historical Context

Before examining local government developments in recent years, it is important to understand the historical context for the current modernisation programme. Collins (1987) describes the Local Government Act 1898 as a frequently neglected watershed in the development of Irish democracy. The 1898 Act transferred various powers to elected councils and widened the franchise to include qualified women. The reforms strengthened the county as a governing entity in Ireland. However, the local government system was still essentially one determined by imposing the British model on Ireland. Following independence, the local government system was overhauled and restructured in the 1920s 'leaving it very largely neither Victorian nor British' (Roche, 1982).

Sheehy (2003) states that 'by the time that independence came, local government was tainted by suggestions of nepotism, corruption, administrative abuse and inefficiency. These difficulties led to tensions with central government which responded in many cases by dissolving the recalcitrant local authority and appointing a commissioner (or commissioners) to run its affairs'. The post-1922 local administration programme, as noted by Roche (1982) pruned away many of the smaller bodies, set up the Local Appointments Commission, started a unified staff service and began to introduce city and county management.

City and county management has been described by Basil Chubb (1983) as one of Ireland's major innovations in the field of government. The idea of city and county management, adapted from American cities, (see Collins, 1987 and Sheehy, 2003, for more details), was first applied to Cork with the passing of the Cork City Management Act, 1929. Dublin followed a year later and the management concept was extended in stages across local government. The County Management Act, 1940 extended the principles of city management to county councils.

Central to the operation of city and county management is the distinction between reserved and executive functions. Reserved functions are those reserved for direct performance by the elected members. Sheehy (2003) states that reserved functions fall into five main categories: finance, legislation, political affairs, policy decisions and control of the executive branch. Executive functions, which are the preserve of the manager, cover day-to-day decisions based on established policy (Asquith and O'Halpin, 1998). Executive functions include issues such as the appointment and control of staff, granting of planning permission and letting of houses.

This emphasis on a strong management role in local government is one of a number of distinguishing features that characterise Irish local government in comparison with local government in many other countries. This strong management role has also been the focus of some discussion and debate concerning the respective roles and power of the manager and elected members. Some commentators have noted a belief that, in practice, the manager occupies the dominant position in local government (see, for example, Zimmerman, 1976). Another characteristic of the manager system is the way managers are recruited and appointed through a centralised Local Appointments Commission, rather than the local authorities themselves choosing the officials selected.

A further distinguishing characteristic of local government in Ireland is the relatively limited range of functions undertaken by local authorities. Traditionally, local services in Ireland are broken down into eight programme groups, as illustrated in Table 2.1. By way of comparison, many local authorities in other OECD countries have responsibility for a much broader range of social services, including primary and secondary education, health, social welfare, care of the elderly and childcare services, public transport, policing and local economic development (Callanan, 2003a).

Table 2.1 Irish local government service programmes

1. Housing and Building	Assessment of the adequacy of housing and the enforcement of minimum standards; management and provision of local authority housing; assistance to persons housing themselves or improving their houses; Traveller accommodation; administration of the social housing options.
2. Road Transportation and Safety	Construction, improvement and maintenance of roads; public lighting; traffic management; road safety education; collection of motor taxation; licensing of drivers, taxi and hackney licensing.
3. Water Supply and Sewerage	Public water supply and sewerage schemes; group schemes; public conveniences.
4. Development and Incentives and Controls	Physical planning policy; control of new development and building; development and implementation of a housing strategy; promotion of industrial and other development; urban and village renewal.
5. Environmental Protection	Waste management; burial grounds; safety of structures and places; fire protection; pollution control; Local Agenda 21; litter control.
6. Recreation and Amenity	Swimming pools; libraries; parks; open spaces; recreation centres; art galleries; museums; theatres; preservation and improvement of amenities.
7. Agriculture, Education, Health and Welfare	Appointments to vocational educational committees, regional health boards, joint drainage committees; administration of higher education grants.
8. Miscellaneous Services	Financial management and rate collection; elections; coroners and inquests; consumer protection measures; abattoirs; corporate estate.

Because of the limited range of functions undertaken, Irish local government expenditure as a proportion of public expenditure and of GNP is low compared with many other European countries (Dollard, 2003). A further distinguishing feature of local government finance is that local government in Ireland has little in the way of tax-raising powers compared to common practice in many other European countries, particularly since the abolition of domestic rates in 1978. In 1997, 'local taxes (in the form of commercial rates) made up just 2.1 per cent of the total share of government taxation. This compares with an average 12.7 per cent across the OECD industrialised countries' (Callanan, 20003b).

A limited local tax base is not necessarily directly correlated with strong central control of local government. Dollard (2003) notes that 'the Netherlands is an example of a viable system of local government based almost entirely on grant finance with local taxes representing less than 10 per cent of income'. However, in the Irish case 'centralisation is strongly imbued within Irish administration culture' (Callanan, 2003b). Haslam (2001) for instance, remarks that the relationship between central government and local government has evolved as one of principal and agent rather than as a partnership.

2.2 Recent developments in Irish local government[1]

Since the early 1990s, there have been a number of significant changes in local government. The period from 1991 to 1994 saw the law in relation to local government being significantly modernised. This includes the granting of a power of 'general competence' (replacing the *ultra vires* doctrine) to local authorities under the Local Government Act 1991, and the establishment of new county councils in Dublin under the Local Government (Dublin) Act, 1993.

The 1980s and 1990s saw an increase in the number of agencies and community groups operating at county level,

[1] *This section draws heavily from an annual review of local government which is published in* Administration *as part of an annual review of public sector developments (see Boyle et al.)*

but not under the aegis of local authorities. This is particularly the case with regard to local development, including groupings such as county enterprise boards, ADM (Area Development Management) partnerships and LEADER rural development groups. These agencies, set up with the support of EU structural funding, were established through government departments as separate, independent entities rather than within local government. The potential for lack of co-ordination and local control of these bodies led governments in the 1990s to promote the local authority as the focus for co-ordinating the activities of local development agencies. In particular, a Devolution Commission was established in 1995 to advise the government on the devolution of functions and responsibilities to local government and on widening the role of local government. In 1996, an interim report was produced by the Devolution Commission. This report, among other things, recommended that local authority and local development systems should be brought together and simplified.

Most significantly from the point of view of this study, December 1996 saw the publication of *Better Local Government – A Programme for Change* (BLG). BLG should be seen in the context of public service modernisation initiatives generally. In 1994 the government announced the Strategic Management Initiative (SMI) for the Irish public service. At central government level, the SMI led to the development of a programme of change for the civil service (Boyle and Humphreys, 2001). Similarly, in the health sector there have been significant management and policy reforms. BLG is thus part of a wider government agenda of change for the public service. BLG is based on four principles:

- enhancing local democracy and widening participation
- serving the customer better
- developing efficiency in local government, and
- providing proper resources to allow local government fulfil the role assigned to it.

A number of key themes underly these principles and

are addressed in some detail in BLG:

- *Strengthening democracy:* Local government to be recognised constitutionally and Ireland to ratify the European Charter of Local Self-Government. An enhanced role for councillors is proposed through the mechanism of Strategic Policy Committees (SPCs), to be established in each county, city and larger urban authority. The chairpersons of these committees, with the chairperson of the council, are to form a corporate policy group, and local interests to have representation on the SPCs. This emphasis on an enhanced role for councillors is aimed at achieving a better balance of power in the relationship between the elected members and the manager, in favour of the elected members.
- *Widening the role of local government:* Councils to appoint directors of community and enterprise development. Community and enterprise groups of the councils to include members drawn from local development bodies. Plans for integration of local government and local development to be prepared.
- *Improving the quality of service:* Performance indicators to be used. High level local project teams to be established to develop proposals for one-stop-shops. A quality award scheme to be introduced and a comprehensive list of public rights to information from local authorities published.
- *Paying for local government:* The full yield from motor taxation to become a dedicated local authority revenue resource.
- *The human resource dimension:* A new management tier to be created in local authorities with clear responsibility for individual programmes and a leading role in servicing the SPCs. A Local Government Management Services Board to be created.
- *Organisation:* County and city authorities to remain the principal units of local government, but action recommended to take account of co-operative efforts between authorities, to encourage decentralisation to area level and to address service delivery issues where

boundaries intersect. Greater co-operation between towns and counties is envisaged.

Subsequent to BLG, the Devolution Commission produced its second report in 1997. This report recommends that devolution should result in the widest possible role for local authorities in relation to specific functional areas where the individual or the local community benefits from local delivery of services. The Commission also recommends that local authorities be developed as genuine multi-purpose bodies with relationships with a wide range of government departments and other agencies, becoming the focus for development within a county. This is in line with the government policy outlined above on making local government the focus of local development initiatives. With regard to this latter point, in 1998 the government established a task force on local government and local development systems. This task force was charged with drawing up a model for the integration of the local government and local development systems. The task force recommended that a new shared vision and strategy covering a ten year period be articulated for each county and city. The task of developing and implementing this vision and strategy is allocated to county/city development boards (CDBs), involving all the main stakeholders at local level. As part of these new arrangements, the CDBs are serviced by directors of community and enterprise, employed by the local authorities. Local councils must approve the ten year strategies.

The Local Government Act 1998 provides for a new funding regime for local government. From 1999, a new local government fund was established, financed from two sources: an exchequer contribution and the proceeds of motor taxation. This money is ringfenced solely for local government purposes. A distribution model, based on needs and resources, has become the basis for making annual allocations from the local government fund to local authorities.

In 1999 local government was given constitutional recognition:

> The state recognises the role of local government in providing a forum for the democratic representation of local communities, in exercising and performing at local level powers and functions conferred by law and in promoting by its initiatives the interests of such communities (Bunreacht na hÉireann, Article 28A.1).

The full text of Article 28A is set out in Appendix 4. The constitutional amendment also provides for local elections every five years.

The year 2000 saw the publication of *Modernising Government – The Challenge for Local Government* by the Department of the Environment and Local Government (hereafter referred to as *Modernising Government*). This document reviews local government reform to date and sets out further challenges. Local authorities are required to prepare new corporate plans in accordance with guidelines set out in *Modernising Government.*

Also in 2000, the *Programme for Prosperity and Fairness* (PPF), the fifth national agreement between the government and social partners on key pay, economic and social issues was published. In the local authority context, a number of commitments are made under the PPF to push forward local government modernisation. This includes the development and implementation of a performance management system to ensure the implementation of corporate plans and business plans. The PPF also commits local authorities to ensure the implementation of the National Anti-Poverty Strategy at local level and more generally to expand their role in relation to social inclusion initiatives.

More recently, the Local Government Act, 2001 represents a significant legislative milestone for local government in Ireland. To a large extent, the legislation backs up the changes that were underway. The Act provides for:

- the renaming of local authorities as county councils, city councils, town councils and, in some cases, borough councils, replacing terms such as county borough council, corporation, urban district council and board of town commissioners

- general, ceremonial and other functions for a local authority
- more flexible arrangements for joint service provision between local authorities
- a formalised strategic management process in the local authorities, which requires a corporate plan to be produced for the life of the council
- a general ethics framework for staff and councillors
- new rights for media and public access to local authority meetings
- the establishment of an independent local government commission to deal with boundary changes and electoral reviews
- other provisions relating to the new financial management framework, operational procedures, local government audit and the making of bye-laws.

The Act emphasises the policy-determining role of councillors.

Also in 2001, the Council of Europe undertook a review of Irish local government. In 1997, Ireland signed the European Charter of Local Self-Government. The Council of Europe review assessed progress toward adherence to the principles of the Charter (see Callanan, 2003a for details of the Charter). The review report welcomes the developments taking place in Irish local government and recommends further developments, including the continuing strengthening of the political and policy-making role of elected members and an increasing role for Irish local government, especially in the areas of health, education, economic development and social matters. These two issues – the strengthening of political decision making and the widening of the role of local government – are key strands of the reform agenda for local government.

Part 2

Community Leadership

3

Strategic Policy Committees, Area Committees and Corporate Policy Groups – Developing Political Decision Making

3.1 Intention of the modernisation programme

Better Local Government (BLG) (1996) states that: 'To date, local government in Ireland has rarely been accorded a status commensurate with its democratic mandate or been accepted fully as a valid partner in the process of government'. BLG recognises a need to enhance democracy at local authority level as part of the general modernisation of local government. In particular, three broad aims are established in this context: to recognise the legitimacy of local government as a democratic institution; to enhance the electoral mandate within local government; and to broaden involvement in local government.

Recognising the legitimacy of local government is primarily achieved through the formal inclusion of local government in the Constitution in 1999. The other two aims of enhancing the electoral mandate and broadening involvement in local authorities are primarily to be met through the creation and operation of strategic policy committees (SPCs) and area committees. With regard to SPCs, BLG states that:

- Each county and city authority and the larger urban authorities will be required to establish SPCs mirroring the major functions of the local authority.
- The number of SPCs will be tailored to the size of the local authority, but should be between two and five; in the smaller authorities, therefore, each SPC would cover several functional areas.
- Each SPC will be supported by the programme manager (subsequently entitled director of service) for the relevant service who will operate under the general direction of the committee and submit policy review papers for the service or services in question. This will give a clear focus to the work of the committee and allow

it to play a major role in the development of corporate policy and in the local SMI process.

- Within this framework, SPCs can identify particular policy areas for special consideration, arrange for their in-depth examination and report on necessary changes to the full council. The authority's annual report will include material specifically dealing with the work of the SPCs.

As far as enhancing the electoral mandate of members is concerned, SPCs are intended to give councillors a more meaningful role in policy review and development. This is particularly the case in relation to functions of a strategic nature, such as the preparation of development plans and the establishment of priorities for services. With regard to broadening involvement in local government, SPCs are to draw not less than one-third of their membership from relevant sectoral interest groupings such as employers, agriculture representatives, trade unions and community and voluntary sector representatives. The intention here is to mirror at local level the national social partnership model.

With regard to area committees, BLG states:

> Increasingly, local authorities are seeking to decentralise decision making to the area level through the creation of committees based on the electoral area. This process should be encouraged though it would not be appropriate to be prescriptive about it, since much will depend on local circumstances. The creation of area committees should enable operational matters to be discussed at that level, leaving the full council free to discuss issues affecting the whole area and policy issues emanating from the SPC system.

While BLG supports initiatives to decentralise decision making, there is a recognition that area committees are not necessarily suitable for all local authorities and that the pattern of decentralisation might vary depending on local circumstances.

As well as SPCs and area committees, BLG envisages the creation of a corporate policy group (CPG) in each local authority. Chaired by the cathaoirleach, supported by the county/city manager, and made up of the chairpersons of the SPCs, the CPG is to act as a sort of cabinet and provide a forum where policy positions affecting the whole council can be agreed for submission to the full council. The CPG has a coordinating role in relation to the work of SPCs.

In 1999, the Department of the Environment and Local Government (DELG) issued guidelines for the establishment and operation of SPCs (Department of the Environment and Local Government, 1999). These guidelines cover such issues as the role of SPCs and CPGs, composition and participation mechanisms. Appendix 1 of the guidelines summarises the central features of the SPC system and is repeated here in Table 3.1.

In summary, SPCs are intended to strengthen the policy-making role of elected councillors, and to broaden participation in local government through the direct involvement of sectoral interests. In terms of the goal of enhancing democracy, SPCs are intended to impact on both representative and participative democracy.

3.2 *The practice*

3.2.1 Strategic Policy Committees

In April 2001, the DELG conducted a survey on the establishment and operation of SPCs and CPGs. This survey provides baseline data on the operation of SPCs and CPGs. It should be noted, however, that the survey was commissioned very shortly after the director of service posts were put in place. As one of the key tasks for directors of service is to support the SPC process, this needs to be borne in mind when interpreting the survey findings. Table 3.2 summarises the survey information collected concerning SPC type and membership.

It can be seen from Table 3.2 that all county and city authorities have SPCs in place. All authorities have committees dealing with housing, planning and transportation, and all but one having an environment SPC. Just over half of the authorities have an SPC dealing with

Table 3.1 Summary of central features of the SPC system

1.	The role of the strategic policy committees (SPCs) and the corporate policy group (CPG) is to formulate policy proposals, evaluate and report on policy implementation, for consideration and final decision by the full council
2.	A focus on the SPCs' policy-making and strategic role is fundamental to the SPC concept. In their work, SPCs are not concerned with individual representational or operational issues.
3.	The SPC system presents councillors with a prime opportunity to become more involved in policy formulation. It provides a chance to review and optimise committee structures and related procedures, which demands a rationalisation of existing committees and standing procedures.
4.	Each authority will generally have four SPCs, with the option of more in the very largest authorities, if warranted.
5.	SPCs are to be chaired by one of the council members.
6.	SPCs are to have a minimum total membership of nine
7.	A minimum of one third of the members of each SPC is to be drawn from relevant sectoral interests; to provide relevant expertise and advice and allow for a range of inputs in the formulation of policy.
8.	Relevant organisations for each sector will be identified as early as possible, parallel with the drafting of the scheme.
9.	Each sector will select its own nominee(s).
10.	The CPG is to comprise the cathaoirleach of the local authority and the SPC chairs. It is to be chaired by the cathaoirleach. It will be supported by the manager.
11.	Area committees can complement the SPC system. Local operational matters should be assigned to the area committees, as the SPC system will not deal with local representational issues and operational issues.

Source: Department of the Environment and Local Government, 1999

Table 3.2 SPC type and membership

Type of SPC	Authorities that have SPC (%)	Average no. of members on SPC	Membership breakdown		Gender breakdown	
			% Councillors	% Sectoral Representatives	% Female	% Male
Housing	100	11	65	35	25	75
Planning	100	12	65	35	15	85
Environment	97	11	66	34	18	82
Transportation	100	12	65	35	16	84
Recreation/ Culture	56	12	65	35	25	75
Other	41	13	65	35	21	79

recreation/culture. Just under half of all authorities have SPCs created to deal with other issues, for example economic development, finance and general, and local urban and rural development.

On average, each SPC has twelve members, and all authorities have met the requirement that at least a third of the membership be drawn from sectoral interest groups. The gender breakdown varies, with roughly a quarter of the membership of planning and recreation/culture SPCs being female, but with around 15 to 18 per cent of members of the planning, environment and transportation SPCs being female. Given that 15 per cent of those elected to local government in 1999 are women (Muintearas, 2002), these figures would suggest that one of the by-products of involving the sectoral interests in SPCs has been to increase female participation in local government decision making.

With regard to sectoral representation, Table 3.3 gives the breakdown among the different sectors. It can be seen that the community/voluntary/disadvantaged sector has the higher level of representation on SPCs, with roughly a third of all sectoral representation on SPCs. The business/commercial sector has the next highest level of representation. With regard to selection of the sectoral representatives, more than three quarters of local authorities facilitated the selection process for the environment/

Table 3.3 Sectoral representation on SPCs

Sector	Number of representatives	% of total representatives
Agriculture/farming	66	10
Environment/conservation /cultural	102	16
Development/construction	75	12
Business/commercial	110	17
Trade union	67	11
Community/voluntary/ disadvantaged	203	32
Other (including educational, cultural, tourism)	12	2

conservation/cultural sector and for the community/ voluntary/disadvantaged sector. Two thirds of local authorities used the community fora (established for nomination to county and city development boards) as the means of nominating representatives from the community/ voluntary/disadvantaged sector. The Community Workers Co-operative (2002) question the use of the broad-based community fora as the mechanism to represent community and voluntary interests, noting that it can result in equality and anti-poverty interests being further marginalised. As an alternative, they point to the growth of autonomous networks and platforms in some counties that have a specific focus on poverty, equality or social exclusion.

There is no data available from the survey on participation rates of the sectoral representatives or of councillors at SPC meetings. Information obtained from the interviews and site visits for this study suggest that participation rates can vary quite significantly, by local authority and by grouping. Some local authorities have good participation rates overall. In others there are problems with participation of some of the sectoral interests in some committees, and in yet other authorities there are reports of uneven participation of councillors in SPCs. The sheer number of meetings held was mentioned as a factor affecting participation rates by some respondents. So too was the direct relevance of the issues to those participating, and the role of the chair in stimulating the process. Similar themes were noted in responses by county and city managers to the questionnaire issued as part of this study. The need for training supports, particularly for sectoral interest representatives, was noted by several managers.

In terms of the policy issues being addressed by SPCs, the DELG survey asked local authorities to identify the top three priority issues being dealt with by SPCs. The most frequently mentioned priority issues are outlined in Table 3.4. While this obviously only gives a snapshot of the key issues at one particular point in time, it is useful in highlighting the type of issue being discussed at SPCs in their early stages of development.

Information obtained from the interviews and site visits for this study suggest that the range of policy-related issues to be discussed at the various SPCs varies. For some committees, such as housing and environment, there is seen to be a wide range of strategic policy-related issues suitable for discussion and debate. For other committees, such as transportation and recreation/culture, the policy agenda is seen as being narrower in scope. Even for those SPCs with a broad range of topics, some concern was expressed about ensuring a supply of sufficient policy-relevant items over the medium to longer term. Some concerns were also expressed concerning the depth of engagement with policy issues. For some SPCs, meetings would only last an hour or so, agendas would only be sent out immediately before the meeting and the degree of meaningful engagement with policy by participants was questioned.

The views of county and city managers on the engagement of SPCs with policy and on the interaction between councillors and sectoral interest representatives are given in Table 3.5, derived from the questionnaire issued to all county and city managers as part of this study. It can be seen that roughly 40 per cent feel that SPCs are

Table 3.4 Top three priority issues being dealt with by SPCs – as of April 2001

Housing	Homelessness strategy Housing strategy – Part V Traveller accommodation
Planning	County/city development plan Housing strategy – Part V Planning and Development Act 2000
Environment	Waste management Litter control policy/management/pollution Recycling policy/water quality standards
Transportation	Road safety policy National roads/non-national roads programme Rural transport initiative/corporate plan
Recreation/Culture	Library development Arts plan/strategy Promotion of Irish language

meaningfully engaged in the examination of local strategic policy issues, while 60 per cent feel that SPCs are engaged only a little or a fair amount. Similarly, 40 per cent feel that councillors and sectoral interests are working well together on SPCs to a large extent. In additional written comments, several managers noted that while SPCs had made a slow start, they were now beginning to engage more with policy issues and they would expect things to continue improving in the future.

Also, in terms of engagement with policy issues, one positive factor noted by many interviewees was the increasing role of chairs of SPCs. SPC chairs often report on developments to the full council, and may present policy papers/positions to the council. Chairs are increasingly undertaking such tasks which were previously seen as the role of the county/city manager. However, managers in some local authorities noted that SPC chairs were slow to

Table 3.5 County and city managers' views of SPCs

	Not at all	A little	A fair amount	A lot	Very much	Total
Strategic policy committees are meaningfully engaged in the examination of local strategic policy issues	0%	21%	41%	31%	7%	100%
Councillors and sectoral interest representatives are working well together on strategic policy committees	0%	10%	52%	35%	3%	100%

take up their roles, with the agenda being largely set by the executive.

3.2.2 Area Committees

Of the twenty-nine county and city managers who replied to the questionnaires, two thirds noted that their councils had established area committees. Several others said that the council was in the process of establishing area committees or had plans to do so. Many local authorities have established area committees based on electoral areas or groupings of electoral areas. Dublin City, for example, has five area committees consisting of members of the council covering groupings of each of the eleven local electoral areas. These area committees deal with area issues, area delivery of service, area development and detailed operational and representational matters. Prior to the area committees being established, Dublin City councillors were interviewed in 1998 by officials of the city corporate planning unit about their views on area committees. The general views expressed were very positive, including:

- area committees are an opportunity for councillors to provide leadership and adopt a stronger role in the community

- area committees provide scope for better service delivery with more local involvement of the authority at area level
- local issues will be dealt with at area committee level, thereby allowing the business of the city council to become more policy-oriented
- councillors anticipate a better working relationship with officials who are area based, and who will be accountable for service delivery in the area
- scope for community and business involvement with local offices will be enhanced.

Many of these goals are being accomplished, not only in Dublin, but as indicated in the feedback received during this study, generally across local authorities where area committees have been established. In particular, many respondents noted the benefits of having area committees deal with local issues and representations, leaving the full council with more time to address council-wide and corporate issues.

Area committees have been well received by city and county managers. As Table 3.6 illustrates, approximately two-thirds feel that area committees have succeeded in freeing full council meetings to deal more with council-wide policy issues. They are seen to work very well if supported by fully functioning support structures at the local level.

In terms of limitations to date, some area committees seem to have generated only limited interest among the local public and media. As the local media, in particular, are important in profiling the work of councillors, this can sometimes lead to local issues being reserved to or raised again in the full council, where the media are more likely to be present.

One interesting innovation in terms of the composition of area committees is provided by the experience of Waterford County Council. Here, as well as elected representatives, community representatives have been included on the area committees. It is too early in their operation as yet to assess what the impact of this development is. As with the SPCs, there was some initial uncertainty among

Table 3.6 County and city managers' views of area committees

	Not at all	A little	A fair amount	A lot	Very much	Total
Area committees have succeeded in freeing full council meetings to deal more with council-wide policy issues	5%	5%	25%	20%	45%	100%

both elected members and the community representatives as to the precise role of the community representatives. To address this issue, separate training workshops were run by officials for councillors and community representatives, and a joint workshop for both groups together held in the autumn of 2002.

3.2.3 Corporate Policy Groups

With regard to corporate policy groups (CPGs), the DELG survey asked a number of questions as summarised in Table 3.7.

It can be seen from Table 3.7 that at the time of the survey, CPGs had only made a limited impact in many local authorities. The responsibilities of the CPG had been agreed by the council in around two thirds of the authorities. CPGs had been reasonably active in addressing specific policy issues facing the council, having done so in 70 per cent of cases. The types of policy issues addressed varied considerably and included items such as BLG staffing and structure proposals, housing strategy, office accommodation and strategic planning guidelines. CPGs have been less active in identifying policy issues to be addressed by SPCs and in making policy proposals to the council based on SPC proposals. In the latter case, making policy proposals to the council, in many cases individual SPC reports and recommendations may go directly to the

Table 3.7 Role of the CPG

	Yes	No
Have the responsibilities of the CPG been agreed by the council?	20 (63%)	12 (37%)
Has the CPG addressed specific policy issues facing the council?	23 (70%)	10 (30%)
Has the CPG identified particular policy issues for the SPCs?	7 (22%)	25 (78%)
Has the CPG made policy recommendations to the council based on SPC proposals?	8 (24%)	26 (76%)

council, limiting the role of the CPG in these matters.

There was quite a wide division in the views of county and city managers on the operation of CPGs, as illustrated in Table 3.8. Here it can be seen that almost a third of managers feel that the CPG is only a little or not at all acting as a forum for giving direction to council priorities, discussing progress and informing members on key policy issues. Conversely, a quarter feel that CPGs are very much acting as a positive forum. Those managers with a positive experience of CPGs often added written comments about the effective forum CPGs provide for highlighting policy issues and developing approaches to dealing with those issues and for discussing possibilities prior to full council.

3.3 Key issues emerging and suggestions for future developments

Arising from this brief review of practice with regard to the operation of SPCs, area committees and CPGs, it can be seen that some progress has been made towards the aims stated when establishing these fora. In terms of enhancing the electoral mandate of local government, more time is being given to policy development and review of strategic issues such as road safety policy, homelessness strategy and litter control. Councillors are being given the opportunity to engage in a more in-depth manner with relevant local policy issues. The chairs of SPCs, rather than the county/city manger, are often presenting policy issues

Table 3.8 County and city managers' views of CPGs

	Not at all	A little	A fair amount	A lot	Very much	Total
The corporate policy group is acting as a forum for giving direction to council priorities, discussing progress and informing members on key policy issues	3%	28%	28%	17%	24%	100%

arising from the SPC at the full council meetings. With regard to broadening involvement in local government, sectoral interest groups make up the one third of SPC membership, as was targeted in BLG. Sectoral interests are making a more structured input to policy deliberations via the SPCs.

However, a number of issues have emerged from this review that will need to be addressed if SPCs, area committees and CPGs are to continue to evolve as intended. In particular, the extent of the real engagement of SPCs with local strategic policy issues varies across local authorities, between SPCs, and among the different groupings represented on SPCs. Several respondents interviewed warned of the danger of SPCs evolving into 'talking shops' with limited relevance to the actual work of local authorities. Two issues in particular emerge as key to the future development of SPCs: the range and supply of policy issues and the level of participation and engagement of elected members and sectoral interests. Other issues relate to the future role of area committees and CPGs.

3.3.1 The range and supply of policy issues to SPCs

The differences between SPCs in terms of the range of policy issues seen as relevant to them was raised in section 3.2.1. It was noted that some SPCs, such as housing, seem to have a broader base of policy issues to draw from than others, such as transportation. The continuing supply of relevant policy issues to all SPCs over the longer-term was raised as an issue of concern. However, in this context it should be noted that in Kerry, where SPCs have been in operation since 1999 (longer than most other authorities), the supply of policy issues to SPCs has not emerged as a problem.

In terms of the range of policy issues to be addressed at SPCs, some respondents suggest that consideration should be given to ensuring that SPCs consider issues that have a local dimension but which are wider than the brief of the council, for example food safety and education issues. In this context, SPCs could be seen as being involved in the process of local needs identification, and determining how the local authority should subsequently work with others to address these needs. The county and city strategies for economic, social and cultural development drawn up by the CDBs (see section 4.2.1) provide a useful starting point for the identification of such issues.

In terms of the supply of policy issues to SPCs, BLG identifies the support role of directors of service in giving focus to the work of the SPCs and submitting policy review papers. Some respondents in the local authorities visited for the study identified the need to develop a research capacity and capability to support directors of service in fulfilling this role. This is being done in various ways. Community and enterprise development officers are a source of research capacity. In Westmeath, the county manager has assigned responsibility to middle management (senior executive officers, senior engineers, county librarian etc) for particular strategic objectives arising from the corporate plan and for ensuring that meaningful policy issues related to these objectives are raised at the SPCs. The issue of research capacity more generally is taken up in more detail in section 4.3.2.

3.3.2 Participation in and engagement with SPCs

The level of participation in SPCs varies. There is no clear pattern to this variation, with some of the authorities interviewed noting problems with attendance by councillors and others noting problems with the attendance of the sectoral representatives. The degree of engagement between councillors and the sectoral representatives was also noted as varying, working well in some committees and less so in others. With regard to the representatives of the community/voluntary/disadvantaged sector in particular, questions were sometimes raised as to the 'representativeness' of these representatives and the degree of feedback between them and the sector on an ongoing basis. Tensions were sometimes mentioned between the role played by sectoral interests in representing the local community as they see it and the representative role of councillors, democratically elected to represent the views of their constituents. To a large extent, the degree to which such issues are a problem in practice often largely comes down to the nature of the personalities involved. The need for continuing training and development supports to facilitate closer inter-working, and to enhance the knowledge of sectoral interest representatives of the working of local government, were seen by many respondents as vital in supporting participation initiatives.

The attendance issue is most likely tied in with the range and nature of policy issues discussed above. The more issues are seen as of practical relevance to those involved, the stronger the incentive to attend. The issues of engagement and representativeness with the sectoral interests suggests that the nomination and feedback process involved for the sectoral representatives should be kept under scrutiny. For the community/voluntary/disadvantaged sector, the role of the community fora could be developed and strengthened, with more explicit links to emerging community networks and platforms focused specifically on social inclusion.

3.3.3 Key elements in the success of SPCs

A number of items emerge which suggest themselves as important determinants in whether or not SPCs are successful:

- The role of the chair of the SPC. The chair has a vital

role in setting the tone for the operation of the SPC. Chairs should engage with the substantive content issues, facilitate interaction between councillors and the sectoral representatives, and establish links with the full council.

- The supply of meaningful policy issues. Here, the role of council staff, and in particular the directors of service, in ensuring relevant papers/background material is crucial. The development of research capacity and capability within the local authority to enable policy issues to be explored is an important factor here.
- The engagement of councillors. The number and timing of meetings can be important, given the overall number of meetings attended. So too is ensuring that councillors can see the linkage between policy discussions and the delivery of services to their constituents.
- The engagement and legitimacy of sectoral representatives. Ensuring that the appointment of sectoral representatives is as representative as practicable and that there is regular feedback between the sector and the representative enhances the legitimacy of the role. Educating representatives on the role and workings of local government is also an important factor.

3.3.4 Area committees

In general terms, area committees have been a welcome development in terms of extending local representative democracy. The intention is to empower local councillors by creating a situation where local decisions are informed by local representatives who have a good local knowledge and who are locally accountable. This is an important process in Ireland where, on average, local authorities are relatively large and cover a larger population compared to many other countries (Callanan, 2003b).

In County Waterford, this extension of representative democracy has been accompanied by an extension of participatory democracy through the inclusion of community representatives on the area committees. This is an interesting innovation worth tracking to assess its implications. Experience from Britain with extending participatory democracy in a similar manner shows many benefits, but also the potential for problems, including the empowerment of some individuals or groups at the expense of others who are left out of the process. As Burns, Hambleton and Hoggett (1994) state:

> Our conclusion is that a key task for area based participatory structures in urban neighbourhoods is to assemble the preconditions from which genuine forms of empowerment can proceed. This involves not only developing the ability of local people to engage in social action, but also furthering the community's capacity to understand different points of view, contain anxiety and rise above sectionalism. These are, by any standards, challenging tasks.

Further key factors in the longer-term success of area committees are the extent to which service provision is decentralised and the effectiveness of interaction between area committees and area offices and officials. The issue of decentralised service delivery is explored in more detail in Chapter 9.

3.3.5 The Corporate Policy Group

As mentioned above in section 3.2.3, CPGs had a limited impact in many local authorities at the time of the DELG survey. From discussions with authorities such as Galway City and Westmeath, where CPGs are seen to be running well, the CPG: meets prior to council meetings and acts as a sounding board to discuss issues, particularly contentious issues, before they appear at full council; is a useful forum for giving direction, discussing progress and in general keeping members up to date on how things are progressing; and enables members to be better informed of the various aspects of particular policy issues. Key to the success of the CPG is the openness of managers and members to working together, and how good members are at feeding back information to their own parties about the discussions at the CPG meetings.

4

Local Government and Local Development – Widening the Influence of Local Government

4.1 Intention of the modernisation programme

At the time *Better Local Government* (BLG) (1996) was published, the government had recognised the absence of co-ordination among the various centrally determined local development initiatives established during the 1980s and early 1990s, such as LEADER groups, partnership companies and county and city enterprise boards. As noted in section 2.2, in the 1990s government policy was to promote the local authority as the primary co-ordinator of local development activities. As also noted in Chapter 2, in 1995, to further this aim, the government appointed a Devolution Commission to make recommendations on the development of a phased programme of devolution of significant additional functions to local government and to advise on the role of local government in the local development process. The Commission published an Interim Report in 1996 and a Second Report in 1997. The Interim Report put particular emphasis on the need to integrate and simplify local government and local development systems and give local government a greater role in local development issues. The Second Report put forward the view that possibilities for devolution should be considered from across the total range of public services where there is local delivery of those services. The stated intention was that local authorities should become genuine multi-purpose bodies and the focus for local development. The Commission indicated the need for strong commitment at both political and administrative level in key central government departments and in local authorities, if significant devolution of functions to local government were to occur.

Also in 1995, county/city strategy groups, were created under the EU structural funds related Operational Programme for Local, Urban and Rural Development 1994-

1999. These groups, chaired by the county or city manager, were intended to co-ordinate local development activity within local authority areas. BLG recognised the need to build on this initiative and to plan for an integrated local government and local development system when the 1994-1999 round of EU structural funds supports ended. Consequently, a Task Force on Integration of Local Government and Local Development Systems was established, and reported in 1998 (Department of the Environment and Local Government, 1998). The Task Force report highlights a need for a shared long-term vision to guide the activities of public sector agencies and initiatives at local level and a new integrated framework based on the city/county. Arising from this process, a number of actions were agreed by government:

- The establishment of county/city development boards (CDBs) to replace the county/city strategy groups. The primary function of the board is to draw up and work towards the implementation of a strategy for economic, social and cultural development for the county/city covering a ten-year period. A key task is bringing about more co-ordinated delivery of local public services.
- The CDBs to be chaired by a local government councillor, with representation from local government at both political and official level, the social partners including the community and voluntary sector, the local development agencies, and relevant state agencies operating at local level.
- CDBs to be supported by the appointment by each local authority of a director of community and enterprise and associated support staff.

The Task Force report also envisaged local authorities taking a greater role in fostering social inclusion as part of its local development remit. This point was emphasised in the *Programme for Prosperity and Fairness* (2000) which states that local authorities will continue to expand their role in social inclusion and work to embed the National Anti-Poverty Strategy in their policies and actions. *Building an Inclusive Society* (2002), the revised National Anti-

Poverty Strategy, indicates that local authorities will develop social inclusion strategies at local level which will influence in particular the operation of strategic development objectives agreed by CDBs.

The broad intention of these moves is to give local government a much stronger role in influencing and co-ordinating local development initiatives, including social inclusion efforts. It is envisaged that local authorities will be centrally placed to lead and secure effective local policies and the delivery of local public services across agencies.

4.2 The practice

In reviewing practice, four main items are assessed: the development of strategies for economic, social and cultural development; the role of directors of community and enterprise and support staff; social inclusion; and an overview of the changing role of local government.

4.2.1 Creating strategies for economic, social and cultural development

By the end of 2002, all county and city development boards had published their strategies for economic, social and cultural development. A review of these strategies notes that, overall, CDBs have published competent, well presented and timely strategies, achieving a degree of consensus on the needs of counties and cities (Fitzpatrick Associates/ERM Ireland, 2002)

Authorities and local communities are now engaged in the implementation of the strategies. A significant challenge here is to ensure that implementation processes and structures are put in place to achieve the desired strategies. In Galway City, co-ordinating groups, each headed by different agencies, are charged with progressing issues. In Kerry, sub-committees have been established to drive the strategies forward, each of which is chaired by a director of service from the local authority.

Another challenge in terms of implementation is to ensure the long-term 'buy-in' to the strategies on the part of local development agencies, state agencies and the sectoral interests. Several respondents in the course of this study noted varying degrees of commitment on the part of the different organisations involved. A couple of the managers noted that local government can only co-ordinate effectively if the various players are willing to share information and work together in a meaningful way. To this end, they saw it as essential that the co-ordinating role is seen as a government priority and that this message is emphasised across all government departments and agencies. This need for central government buy-in is also strongly emphasised in the Fitzpatrick Associates/ERM Ireland (2002) review of CDB strategies, which states that '... for the central level, the key message of the strategies is that the local service integration mission will ultimately be as successful or unsuccessful as central government organisations wish it to be'.

4.2.2 The role of directors of community and enterprise and associated support staff

BLG and *Modernising Government* envisaged that county and city development boards would be facilitated by directors of community and enterprise and associated support staff, appointed by local authorities. Indeed, in those authorities where the CDB is seen to be operating well and with a good strategy, the role of the director of community and enterprise in supporting and driving the process is seen as a vital element in that success.

The directors of community and enterprise are themselves assisted by support staff. Local authorities have established community and enterprise units with support staff, including community and enterprise development officers. These support staff have played an important role in facilitating the development of the county and city strategies for economic, social and cultural development. They have also helped in the creation of a research resource within local authorities. For example, Kerry County Council made a submission in response to a Department of Public Enterprise rail strategy document. The drafting of this submission was carried out by the community and enterprise staff. In the past, the authority would have been interested in the issue but may not have had the capacity to respond.

4.2.3 Social inclusion

Social inclusion issues feature prominently in the strategies for economic, social and cultural development. The single largest group of actions identified in strategies relate to the social inclusion sector (Fitzpatrick Associates/ERM Ireland, 2002).

Directors of community and enterprise are key players in promoting social inclusion in local authorities. An analysis of local social partnerships by the Community Workers Co-operative (2001) notes that some directors of community and enterprise have set up internal social inclusion working groups within the local authorities. They also note that the individual style and objectives of the directors seems to greatly influence the social inclusion focus of authorities.

In nine local authorities, social inclusion units have been established. This is part of the rolling out of the National Anti-Poverty Strategy at local level as agreed in the PPF (the roll out of the units was implemented in tandem with the launch of the RAPID (Revitalising Areas by Planning, Investment and Development) programme – see below for details). These social inclusion units, normally comprising a social inclusion officer and a social inclusion analyst, have a number of roles:

- fact-finding, identifying the baseline data on the extent, nature and causes of poverty within a county or city – this includes developing local poverty profiles and establishing what is being done in terms of social inclusion work locally;
- promoting social inclusion within the local authority through training and information;
- co-ordinating the various agencies working to tackle poverty and disadvantage both within councils and the wider community (and working in particular with the social inclusion measures groups formed by the county and city development boards);

- monitoring and evaluating the impact of actions and policies (Allen, 2001).

In particular areas of disadvantage, the government has established special programmes to advance investment, which impact on the work of local authorities in these areas. The RAPID (Revitalising Areas by Planning, Investment and Development) programme is overseen by the Department of Community, Rural and Gaeltacht Affairs and managed by ADM Ltd. on behalf of the department. RAPID is composed of two strands, one targeted at twenty-five urban centres, the other targeted at twenty provincial towns, each of which were identified as having the greatest concentration of disadvantage. The areas receive priority funding under the National Development Programme, on the basis of plans drawn up locally.

As well as the RAPID programme, in 2000 the government launched the CLÁR (Ceantair Laga Ard Riachtanais) programme designed to address rural areas of special disadvantage. This programme is also co-ordinated by the Department of Community, Rural and Gaeltacht Affairs, in this case in association with the county development boards. It operates in sixteen areas, selected as those which have suffered the greatest depopulation since 1926, plus the Cooley peninsula.

A further aspect of note with regard to social inclusion is the central support role played by the Combat Poverty Agency (CPA). In co-operation with the DELG and the National Anti-Poverty Strategy unit, the CPA has established a local government anti-poverty learning network. This network aims to (a) provide a forum where local authorities can share experience and consider how to develop policies to address social exclusion, and (b) support and assist local authorities to incorporate a strong anti-poverty focus within their work. The network, which thirty of the thirty-four city and county authorities had opted to join by November 2002, provides seminars/workshops, training, advice and support, a newsletter, a pilot project on poverty profiling, and a local government anti-poverty initiatives grants scheme. The budget for the network for 2002 was €380,000. An initial review of the network found that most participants see it as a positive development. The main strengths of the network are that it provides good examples of practice, an opportunity to network and good training on relevant topics. The main weakness is that it is seen, to some degree, to be preaching to the converted, i.e. those already involved in social inclusion work (Fitzpatrick Associates, 2002).

4.2.4 Overview of the changing role of local government

Table 4.1 summarises the views of county and city managers on some aspects of local government and local development. Overall, there is strong support for the statement that local government now has a stronger role in influencing and co-ordinating local development initiatives. Several managers added, in written comments, that the local authority is now seen as a significant player with a higher profile. Similarly, social inclusion is generally seen as having more prominence now in local authorities than in the past.

However, with regard to the other aspect of the work of the Devolution Commission, the progression of the devolution of functions to local government, there has been little change in the balance of functions between central and local government levels. In introducing the Local Government Bill 2000 (later to become the Local Government Act 2001) to the Dáil, the then Minister for the Environment and Local Government, Noel Dempsey TD, stated:

> Local government in any country derives from the particular tradition, history, culture and circumstances of that country and prospects for change must bear this in mind. The delivery of functions such as policing, public transport, health and social welfare, comes within the local government system in some other countries. However, if we are realistic, given current Irish circumstances, it is unlikely that in the short term these will be subsumed within our local government system or that there is a demand for such, much as we might wish it so. In short, if local government is to

Table 4.1 County and city managers' views on local government and local development

	Not at all	A little	A fair amount	A lot	Very much	Total
Local government has a stronger role now in influencing and co-ordinating local development initiatives	0%	3%	21%	48%	28%	100%
Social inclusion is a more prominent item on the local authority agenda than in the past	3%	3%	38%	41%	14%	100%
The local authority is seen by the public as the leader of local development initiatives in the area	0%	7%	35%	41%	17%	100%

progress in this country, it demands that we approach change in a realistic way taking account of how functional responsibilities have evolved and how they are currently organised (*Dáil debates*, Vol. 532, Col. 831).

Instead of a focus on devolving further functions to local government, in practice the emphasis has been on increasing the role of local government in co-ordinating the activities of public bodies at local level.

4.3 Key issues emerging and suggestions for future developments

It can be seen that there has been a significant amount of activity in the area of local government and local development. Local strategies and structures are now in place to address economic, social and cultural development. Social inclusion features significantly in the strategies and in other actions being undertaken at local level, such as the RAPID and CLÁR programmes and across local authorities generally. In broad terms, the CDB system seems to be well accepted, and the directors of community and enterprise and community and enterprise units are now becoming an integral part of the local government system. The challenge in the next phase is to move on to the implementation of the strategies to deliver practical benefits in terms of local development.

Before going on to examine the implications of this implementation challenge, it is worth considering what has led to the progress made to date. One particular feature, noted by many respondents to this study, is the degree of structural supports given to the local government and local development initiative. Three aspects of these structural supports are worth particular mention. First is the Task Force on Integration of Local Government and Local Development Systems, chaired by the Minister for the Environment and Local Government. The task force has been particularly helpful in overseeing activity and in involving key actors from the main government departments in the process. Second, the creation of the post of director of community and enterprise and the creation of community and enterprise units within local authorities has given a specific focus to local government and local development work, largely through the CDBs. This has greatly facilitated the development of a co-ordination role in terms of local development by the local authority. Third, within the field of social inclusion, the support provided by the Combat Poverty Agency through the local anti-poverty learning network has been of value. The network is particularly useful in terms of exchange of information and the dissemination of good practice. These lessons regarding the role of structural supports in promoting modernisation have implications more generally across local government.

With regard to next steps and new challenges, three issues in particular arise from the review of progress to date: the increasing role of local government in local governance issues; the development of research capacity within local authorities; and the need for evaluation and scrutiny of the complex web of local initiatives.

4.3.1 The role of local government in promoting local governance

With the development of CDBs, directors of community and enterprise etc, local authorities are, as envisaged, playing a more central co-ordinating role in local development issues. But there are still a wide range of actors involved, including national and local agencies, the public, and the private, voluntary and community sectors. Local authorities are but one body amongst many involved in local development. The Community Workers Co-operative (2001) note scepticism about the degree of 'buy-in' to the process, particularly in middle and lower management in some public bodies. CDBs need to continue to strengthen their position with regard to ensuring implementation within the local government system and in the wider local environment. In this setting, local governance issues gain greater prominence. As Wilson (2000) notes: 'whereas local government is concerned with the formal institutions of government at the local level, local governance focuses upon the wider processes through which public policy is shaped in localities. It refers to the development and implementation of public policy through a broader range of public and private agencies than those traditionally associated with elected local government'. Similarly, Quinlivan (2001) notes that there are issues such as urban regeneration and public safety which face local authorities but which do not fit conventional organisational boundaries or traditional ways of working: 'in simple terms, these are issues which are not owned by any one bit of a local authority and also they are not solely the preserve of the local authority. New creative approaches and fresh ways of thinking are required to meet these challenges'.

If local authorities are to be seen as taking the lead in co-ordinating the development and implementation of local development and local public service activities, they also need to be seen as leading the move to better local governance. This requires action both within local authorities and across the various agencies involved. Within local authorities, there needs to be widespread understanding of the need for a shared understanding of and commitment to the main governance issues. To take social inclusion as an example, it is imperative that social inclusion is not seen as a responsibility of a social inclusion unit/the community section alone. The actions of all parts of the authority impact on social inclusion. Similarly, across organisational boundaries, local authorities have a role in leading the public service changes required at local level. The kind of issues this raises are set out in Table 4.2, abstracted from work by Bovaird and Löffler (2002).

A further challenge to local government is the periodic pressure put on central government to relieve local authorities of some of their existing powers and for new central structures to be developed. An example here is the issue of waste management, where there have been calls to set up a national waste management agency to implement regional waste plans. Unless local authorities can minimise the situation where controversial issues for decision are either referred to the manager or given to a central agency, the case for local government to develop a leadership role locally will be weakened. On the other hand, it is important that national-level policies are designed and delivered in a way that facilitates rather than restricts the local leadership role of local authorities.

4.3.2 The development of research capacity within local authorities

The positive contribution which community and enterprise staff and the social inclusion units have made to enhancing the research capacity of local authorities has been mentioned. In order to co-ordinate appropriate local development strategies, it is necessary to have sound information on which to base the approach adopted and evidence in relation to what is happening in practice. Sanderson, Percy-Smith and Dawson (2001) indicate that research can assist local authorities to:

- understand the social and economic environment in which they are operating, thereby contributing to effective strategy development
- understand the problems and needs of local

Table 4.2 Widening the scope of local government towards 'good local governance'

Local government needs to consider not only ... **Organisational leadership**	*... but increasingly* **Leadership of networks**
Developing organisations Ensuring policy coherence across organisational departments and services Creating a set of values and a sense of direction, which leaves room for individual autonomy and creativity for mid-level managers and employees	Developing communities Ensuring policy coherence across organisational and sectoral borders and levels of government as well as over time (sustainable development) Managing expectations of citizens, companies and other stakeholders so that they become more deeply committed to democratic processes and more engaged in policy making and services management
Functioning of the local authority	**Developing good local governance**
Serving the community by producing policies, services and information ('service provider') Improving the internal efficiency of local authorities Increasing user satisfaction of local services	Enabling the community to plan and manage its own affairs ('community developer') Improving the external effectiveness of local authorities Building public trust in local government through transparent processes and accountability and through democratic dialogue

(Source: abstracted from Bovaird and Löffler, 2002)

communities, thereby leading to effective policies and services

- increase the awareness of alternative ways of doing things as a basis for innovation and change in policy, service delivery and management
- understand the views of local citizens and other stakeholders about the services and activities of the authority
- promote involvement and participation of citizens

- understand the impact of strategies, policies, programmes and services on the well-being of communities and the locality.

However, despite the initial steps being taken in developing a research capacity, this capacity is currently unevenly distributed across local authorities. For example, the development of local poverty profiles is moving slower than expected because many authorities do not have the staff with the relevant skills to develop profiles. And in those authorities which are beginning to build up and use research capacity, they are still very much at the early stages of development. This issue of research capacity was also touched upon in section 3.3.1 in the context of providing useful policy papers for SPCs.

Evidence from local authorities in Britain, where similar research capacity limitations have been experienced, suggest ways forward (Sanderson, Percy-Smith and Dawson, 2001). First, research needs to be planned from a strategic, corporate perspective. Second, there is a need for better co-ordination and rationalisation of information collection, management and use across the organisation, especially when linked in with the development of geographical information systems (GIS). Third, there needs to be an increasing emphasis on collaboration and partnership, working on research with other authorities and agencies, particularly local third-level institutions. And fourth, national local government organisations and central government should take a more active role in supporting the research process at local authority level. With regard to this last point, recent developments in the Local Government Management Services Board to enhance their own research capability available to local government is to be welcomed.

4.3.3 Evaluation and scrutiny of local initiatives

Part of the justification for the enhanced role of local government in local development is to improve co-ordination and avoid overlaps in the complex network of agencies and programmes operating at the local level.

While CDBs and the local strategies have contributed to improved co-ordination, the potential for overlap and lack of focus is still significant. The boundaries and responsibilities for tackling economic, social and cultural issues remain diffuse and somewhat blurred at times. It is therefore important that the efficiency and effectiveness of the system overall in addressing local development issues is kept under constant scrutiny and review. To this end, one particularly significant piece of work will be the evaluation of county and city development boards' role in co-ordinating social inclusion, to be undertaken by the National Development Plan/Community Support Framework evaluation unit in 2003.

Part 3

Efficiency and Effectiveness

5

The Production of Corporate Plans

5.1 Intention of the modernisation programme

As part of the extension of the Strategic Management Initiative (SMI) to the wider public service, local authorities were asked by the Department of the Environment and Local Government (DELG) in March 1996 to develop strategy statements (corporate plans), both in the context of government policy generally and of the DELG's own strategy statement. Subsequently, Modernising Government (2000) stated that local authority strategy statements will be styled as corporate plans, to recognise the business ethos underlying the operation of local authorities. Modernising Government required that corporate plans be produced covering the remaining period of office of the 1999-2004 councils.

The production of corporate plans is legally mandated under the Local Government Act 2001. Section 134 of the Act states that local authorities must produce a corporate plan, normally covering the life of the council. The plan:

> Must set out the principal activities of the local authority, its objectives and priorities, proposals to work towards improved customer service and human resource activities. The plan must be drawn up in consultation with the corporate policy group, in accordance with any Ministerial guidelines, and is adopted by the elected council. An annual progress report must be submitted by the manager. (Local Government Bill, 2000 Explanatory Memorandum).

Modernising Government (2000) contains an appendix setting out guidelines for local authorities on the preparation of corporate plans. These guidelines indicate that elected members and staff should be involved in the process of producing the corporate plan. They also state that the plan must be consistent with the goals and objectives of the Department of the Environment and Local Government, as set out in its strategy statement. Key elements to be incorporated in corporate plans are set out:

- mission statement and mandate
- core objectives and supporting strategies
- operating environment
- citizen/customer focus
- internal capability to realise the goals
- resource allocation/reallocation issues
- implementation and on-going assessment strategy
- monitoring, reporting and corrective action intended.

5.2 The practice

All of the published corporate plans covering the period 2001-2004 were reviewed as part of this study. The production of corporate plans is a relatively new initiative for local authorities. Despite this, corporate plans are viewed very positively by county and city managers, as illustrated in Table 5.1. Over 80 per cent believe that the corporate plan to a large extent prioritises the council's main objectives and gives more of a focus on results. However, in general managers see a need to do more work to secure ownership of the corporate plan by staff.

While the corporate plans represent a useful overview of council intentions, in many cases they can be improved. In the discussion below, the limitations of existing plans, together with examples of good practice, are set out for each of the main elements of the plans.

5.2.1 Mission statement and mandate

Expressing their mission and mandate provides local authorities with an opportunity to set out how they would like to see their county or city develop, and their role in this process. A mission statement can act as a guide to policy and strategy formulation, establishing the broad purpose and values guiding the local authority. Alternatively, a mission statement can simply be produced to meet a requirement, with little real meaning or resonance for

Table 5.1 County and city managers' views of corporate plans

	Not at all	A little	A fair amount	A lot	Very much	Total
The corporate plan usefully prioritises the council's main objectives and gives us more of a focus on results	0%	0%	17%	41%	41%	100%
The corporate plan is widely understood and 'owned' by staff	0%	14%	52%	24%	10%	100%

organisations.

Outlining a mission and associated core values is one of the stronger aspects of local authority corporate plans. Nearly all plans have mission statements that give a short, broad picture of what they want to achieve. This statement is supported by a listing of core values, covering such issues as leadership, customer orientation, equity, sustainability and accountability. However, the real test of all mission, vision and value statements is not the written text itself but the putting into practice of the standard and behaviours contained in the statements.

The manner in which the mandate of the local authority is addressed varies from plan to plan, with some not covering the issue and others going into some depth. Examples of plans where the mandate is addressed relatively well include Kildare, Meath and Offaly.

5.2.2 Description of operating environment

The environmental analysis is a vital element of any corporate plan. The analysis should inform and define the critical issues to be faced in the remainder of the plan. In the case of the local authority plans, many have a tendency to list issues in a rather formulaic manner, rather than draw a linkage between the analysis and subsequent objectives and strategies. There is a sense at times that the 'operating environment' section of the plan is there because it is a requirement of the guidelines rather than a driving element of the strategic management process. In many cases, there is little sense of the main changes taking place in the local authority area with regard to demography, economic and employment patterns, social issues and environmental changes and so on.

In some of the corporate plans where the operating environment issue is more successfully addressed, the analysis aims to identify the main challenges and sets the context for subsequent strategies. The Waterford County plan, for example, in its operating environment analysis highlights notable population trends, changes in labour force composition and mobility as well as issues like the impact of the National Development Plan 2000-2006. Wexford County in its plan identifies key forces for change which will affect the working of the council over the life of the plan.

5.2.3 Elaboration of objectives and strategies

The guidelines set out in *Modernising Government* (2000) indicate that core objectives should be expressed in terms of intended effects or outcomes and should be achievable. Strategies should indicate how these objectives are to be achieved. All the corporate plans outline objectives and strategies. The presentation of these varies. Some authorities, such as Galway City and Kilkenny County, group their objectives and strategies by service programme (e.g. housing and building, recreation and amenity). Others, such as Cork City and Limerick City, group objectives and strategies by Strategic Policy Committees. Yet others, such as Dun Laoghaire-Rathdown and South Dublin, maintain high-level corporate objectives and strategies.

A general criticism of many of the objectives and strategies in the corporate plans is that they tend to be very general and ambiguous statements rather than being focused and targeted. To use the management jargon of the day, many objectives and strategies are insufficiently

SMART (specific, measurable, achievable, realistic and time-related). For example, providing 'appropriate' or 'adequate' facilities or services begs the question of what is appropriate or adequate, and who makes the judgement as to appropriateness and adequacy.

Some plans do have objectives and strategies which are more clear and specific in nature. Kildare, for example, in its objectives for each sector sets out outcomes which it wants to achieve by 2004 (for example 'to substantially reduce the waiting list so that no applicant has to wait more than two years', in the housing construction programme – thus introducing a measurable element of no more than two years on the waiting list to qualify the reference to 'substantial' reductions in this case). Strategies and performance indicators then show how the objectives are to be achieved and assessed. South Dublin sets out outcomes under each of its corporate themes, establishing what is intended to be different by 2006 (for example 'the provision of accurate and timely information on performance against agreed targets of departments and staff' under the resource management theme). The Dun Laoghaire-Rathdown plan contains action plans which specify responsibility and timescale for each of the actions (strategies) outlined in the plan.

5.2.4 Ensuring a citizen/customer focus

This issue of citizen/customer focus is addressed in more detail in the section on quality services, and specifically in the review of customer action plans in Chapter 10. All the corporate plans explicitly recognise the importance of the citizen/customer, with most leaving the specific actions to be undertaken to be elaborated on in their customer action plans. An example of the customer-focused strategies being developed is set out in Table 5.3, taken from Cork County Council's corporate plan. With regard to the corporate planning process itself, there is limited evidence of engagement with the citizen/customer in the production of the corporate plan. Several plans mention their intention to undertake customer surveys and establish customer panels or user groups, but these have not significantly impacted on

Table 5.3 Customer Excellence Strategies

Performance targets in terms of service delivery will be established and progress towards these will be constantly monitored. Specific strategies in the area of customer excellence include:
The setting of quality initiative targets in each major service delivery area. Appropriate performance indicators will be developed and used to monitor resulting progress.
Prioritised enhancement to the quality of service provided in specific service areas.
The creation of a customer panel in major service areas to monitor customer awareness levels, needs and attitudes on a regular basis.
The establishment of a staff-based group to ensure the proper development of our employees who will play the integral part in the future of our organisation.
Training and development of staff who are involved in the front-line provision of services.
Each internal unit of the Council will develop its own objectives in the area of customer service standards.
The Council will seek to achieve Quality Marks in selected service areas.

Source: Cork County Council Corporate Plan 1999-2004

the 2001-2004 corporate plans.

5.2.5 Internal capacity and resource allocation decisions

The guidelines indicate that the corporate plans should set out the internal capacity issues that must be addressed in order to achieve the desired objectives and strategies, including organisational re-structuring. This may involve the re-allocation of resources, both human and financial, in line with identified priorities.

The issues of human resource (HR) capacity and financial management are addressed in more detail in other sections. With regard to the content of the corporate plans themselves, most have objectives and strategies that address HR, financial management and information and communication technology capacity issues. However, a general criticism, similar to that of the objectives and strategies overall, is that these objectives and strategies tend to be highly generalised statements that give little sense of actual prioritisation and the specific actions that are needed. Similarly, the financial resource implications of the totality of objectives and strategies tends not to be addressed, even in a broad manner. It is thus impossible to tell if what is proposed in many cases is well-costed or simply a wish-list.

In terms of good practice in plan content, the Limerick City and Meath corporate plans are examples of plans that have sections on organisational structure and resource development issues. These indicate, in particular, how the council's are re-arranging their organisation in line with corporate plan priorities, as opposed to the traditional programme basis, to meet the new strategic and political policy priorities.

5.2.6 Ensuring implementation and monitoring

The need for indicators of progress, internal management systems and target setting to ensure implementation of the plan and facilitate monitoring of progress is spelt out in the guidelines in *Modernising Government* (2000). In practice, many plans do not contain performance indicators, though in several cases they indicate these will be developed as part of the production of annual operational plans. Of the plans that do contain performance indicators, many of the indicators are vague and ambiguous in nature. Plans which have made a significant attempt to develop indicators that relate to objectives and strategies include Cork City, Dublin City, Galway City, Kildare, Monaghan and Waterford County. An example is given in Table 5.4, drawn from the Kildare corporate plan. The Kildare plan, in an appendix, also outlines activity levels for the year 2000 for various service programmes. These could form the basis for benchmarking progress and changes in demand over the course of the plan.

A further key issue with regard to implementation is the

Table 5.4 Example of Performance Indicator Development

Strategic Issue Key issue facing the council over the next four years	**1. Availability of potable water**	**2. Adequacy of water supply network**
Objective What we want to achieve by 2004	*To source adequate supplies of potable water to meet demand levels*	*To maintain and expand water supply network to meet demand*
Strategies How we are going to achieve our objectives by 2004	• Carry out baseline survey and annual reviews of existing services • Consolidate water supply agreements • Implement water conservation programme • Identify new sources and funding to access same • Provide appropriate treatment	• Implement water strategy to increase supply and treatment • Rolling programme to provide new infrastructure and maintain existing water supply network • Ensure adequacy of private extensions and connections to network • Implement group schemes programme
Performance Measurements How we will know that we have achieved our objectives	• Changes over baseline study • Cost per unit by source • % of samples within statutory requirements • Increase water supply capacity (million litres day) • Dependency on third party supplies • Number of metered commercial consumers • % leakage	• Number of connections/populati on served by public supply • % of population serviced • Number and cost of repairing interruptions in supply • Increase in area served

Source: Kildare County Council Corporate Plan 2001-2004

use of operational plans at programme and division level. While nearly 60 per cent of county and city managers feel that operational plans have significantly helped improve the performance of the authority, 40 per cent feel that operational plans have only contributed a fair amount to performance at this stage. Operational plans are seen as important in prioritising actions and in helping to monitor and measure performance, but they are very much seen as at the early stages of development in most local authorities.

With regard to broader monitoring and implementation issues, some plans set out the procedures they intend to follow regarding monitoring and review of the plan. Both the Dublin City and Meath plans, for example, indicate that quarterly reports on departmental implementation of their annual operational plans will be submitted to a senior management group and/or relevant SPCs and the corporate policy group. The Monaghan and Waterford County plans contain good sections on monitoring and review procedures, establishing a framework for monitoring including the management team, department teams, partnership committee, SPC/CPG, customer feedback, and the elected council.

5.3 *Key issues emerging and suggestions for future developments*

A couple of introductory comments should be made concerning this brief review of corporate plans. First, as stated earlier local authorities are still familiarising themselves with the process involved in producing corporate plans, with the existing plans being only the second iteration. It is likely that improvements will take place over time, as has been the experience of the civil service with strategy statements (see Boyle and Fleming, 2000). Second, this review has focused on the content of the plans themselves. More important in overall terms is the quality of the corporate planning process. Essentially, the plan should be seen as a by-product of a wider process of engagement with strategic issues rather than as the primary end product in and of itself.

Given these points, a number of general priorities

emerge concerning issues that local authorities should be paying attention to as part of their corporate planning process, and in preparation for the next round of corporate plans:

- Ensure that the mission statement and mandate is clear and put into practice in terms of guiding the actions of the local authority. It could be useful to elaborate on the mission, as in the case of the vision for Limerick City (Table 5.2), setting clear outcomes to be achieved or moved towards during the lifetime of the plan. Aim to ensure that staff behaviours mirror the standards and values established.
- In reviewing the operating environment and conducting an environmental analysis, identify significant developments that will impact on the work of the authority in areas such as demographic change, new employment patterns, emerging social problems and issues, changing lifestyles and so on. Review public attitudes towards and needs for services as part of the environmental analysis. And ensure that objectives and strategies clearly flow from the analysis that is undertaken.
- Objectives and strategies should be more clearly defined and specified, and focused on outcomes where possible. Linking objectives and strategies to desired outcomes at a future date (as in Kildare and South Dublin) and specifying responsibility and a timescale for strategy achievement (as in Dun Laoghaire-Rathdown) are suggestions of useful ways forward.
- Citizen/customer expectations and needs should be a major source of strategic issues arising in the corporate plan, with clear linkage to the customer action plans as appropriate. It might be expected that customer surveys, panels etc. referred to in the current plans will be used as key sources of information regarding future developments.
- In further developing and shaping internal capacity, it will be important to match capacity to the strategic priorities identified, ensuring that the capacity exists to

match the aspirations, and vice versa. In a similar light, plans and the planning process should reflect, in broad terms, the resources needed to achieve objectives and strategies.

- Regarding implementation and monitoring, there is a need to develop further the performance indicators being used to assess progress. Practice in the selection and application of indicators should be reviewed so that information needed to manage more effectively is provided. Structural review procedures, such as those proposed by Monaghan and Waterford County, should be put in place and used to track implementation issues. Operational plans should also be further developed as a key implementation mechanism.

As an example of international best practice, and the direction in which local authority corporate plans might increasingly move in the future, abstracts from Manukau City (New Zealand) Strategic Plan 2001-2011 are set out in Figure 5.1 and Table 5.5. Figure 5.1 illustrates a strong focus on improving city outcomes and the contribution of Manukau City Council to the achievement of these outcomes, in terms of citizen, customer and community strategies and in terms of management strategies.

Table 5.5, taking the citizen and customer strategy of developing a safe and attractive city, sets out five year actions and clear, outcome-focused performance targets. This approach is applied to all the strategies contained in the plan.

5.3.1 A key role for annual progress reports

In the context of the implementation of corporate plans, annual progress reports will have an important role to play in tracking developments. Section 134 of the Local Government Act 2001 includes a reference to the requirement for each local authority to submit to the elected members an annual progress report with respect to the implementation of the corporate plan. This progress report should be subsequently detailed in the local authority's annual report. The intention is that the report should be

Figure 5.1

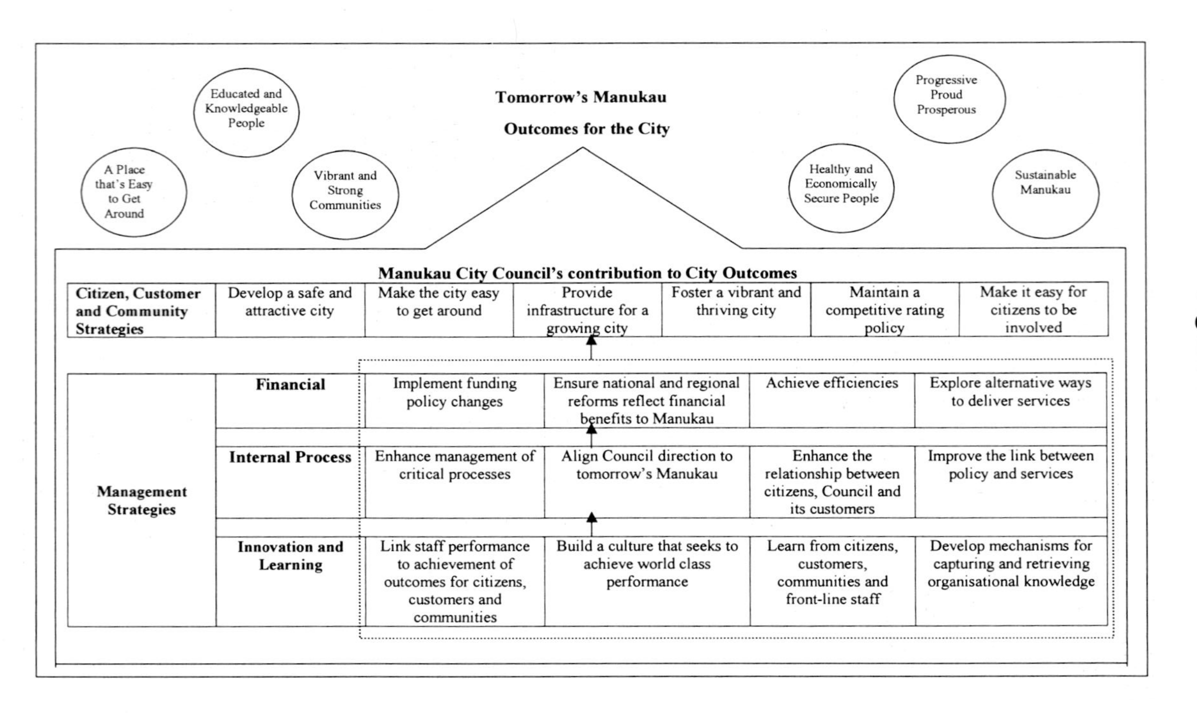

Source: Manukau City Council Strategic Plan 2001-2011

Table 5.5 Council Annual Plan Scorecard to 2006

Five Year Strategies and Targets	Action Over the Next Five Years	Performance Target to 30 June 2002
Citizen and Customer Strategies		
1. Develop a Safe and Attractive City Residents feeling safe in their homes, town centres and neighbourhoods (day and night) increases from 72% to 85% by 2006	1.1 *Improve safety in public places* 2001/02 priorities include: • Upgrade street lights city-wide • Safer Manukau initiatives • Injury Free Counties Manakau initiatives • City and local area development (CLAD) in old Papatoetoe	80% of citizens feel safe where Council has installed safety features over the year
	1.2 *Improve road safety* 2001/2002 priorities include road improvements at: • Ti Rakau/Te Irirangi • Whitford/Maraetai Henson Improvements • Whitford Maraetai Trig • Wellington St/Neilson St Intersection • Pedestrian crossings (city-wide) • Roundabout upgrades (city-wide)	90% decrease in serious-injury traffic incidents where road condition is a factor where Council has made roading improvements this year
	1.3 *Enhance the image of the city* 2001/02 priorities include: • Reducing graffiti • Encouraging volunteers participation in beautification projects • Additional street trees and gardens city-wide	65% of citizens are satisfied with how the city looks and feels where the Council has made improvements over the year Graffiti counts are reduced from an average 579 incidents per quarter in 2000/01 to 550 incidents per quarter in 2001/02 Volunteer groups increases from 92 in 2000/01 to 100 in 2001/02
	1.4 *Provide access to natural environments* 2001/02 priorities include: • Improving public spaces • Puhunui stream • Otara Creek	Citizens' perception that public open space meets community needs improves from 56% in 2000/01 to 60% in 2001/02

Source: Manukau City Council Strategic Plan 2001-2011

used to (a) report on progress with regard to the implementation of the objectives and strategies set out in the corporate plan, and (b) note changes which have taken place which impact on the achievement of objectives and strategies or which call for new objectives and strategies not originally envisaged in the corporate plan.

The first annual reports to address 2001-2004 corporate plans had not been published at the time this review of corporate plans took place in mid-2002. Consequently, it is not possible to comment on their strengths and weaknesses. However, the published annual reports for 2000 were reviewed to give an overview of the current state of performance reporting. Based on this overview, and more importantly on the experience of the civil service regarding the production of annual progress reports on strategy statements (see Boyle, 2001 for details), it would seem that a number of issues will need to be borne in mind when annual progress reports are produced:

- Information presented should be clear and structured, so that progress against the objectives and strategies set out in the corporate plan can be clearly assessed.
- Where possible, reports should not simply be activity and output-based, but also indicate the outcomes arising as a result of the activities undertaken.
- Comparative data should be used, to enable judgements on performance to be put in context. This may be comparing changes over time, against set standards, or other benchmarks. Some local authorities, such as Kerry and Westmeath, already produce some comparative data in their annual reports.
- Reports should present a balanced view of progress, indicating areas where progress has not been made as planned as well as listing achievements.
- Attention should be paid to reviewing the continuing relevance of objectives and strategies to changing circumstances. The annual report should indicate new or changed priorities. The Kerry 2000 annual report, for each service area, usefully lists the main aims for 2001

as well as reviewing progress in 2000.

Building on the information provided concerning Manukau City Council corporate plan above, Table 5.6 outlines an abstract from their 2001 annual report. Here, progress against specified strategies and objectives can be clearly assessed. It provides an example of structured performance reporting with a strong citizen/consumer focus.

Table 5.6 Performance Reporting

Strategy: Contribute towards the reduction of violence and crime and enhance public safety		
Objective	**Measure/Indicator**	**Progress**
Contribute towards the reduction of violence and crime and enhance public safety through advocacy, facilitating access to community facilities, programmes, services and resourcing and reduction of hazards in public places	75% of respondents to a residents' survey perceive they are 'safe' or 'very safe' in areas where Council has actively worked on safety issues.	Overall, the majority of citizens feel safe in their neighbourhood (89%) and their local town centre (91%) during the day. Perceptions reduce significantly after dark with only 58% of citizens feeling safe in their neighbourhood (an increase from 53% in 2000) and 51% feeling safe in their town centre (an increase from 47% in 2000). Manurewa and Papatoetoe town centres were identified as places where people were more likely to feel unsafe after dark. In the past year, Safer Manukau has undertaken a number of safety audits targeted at Otara, Mangere and Papatoetoe wards. These have focused on improvements to street lighting, visibility around public areas, and the eradication of graffiti

Source: Manukau City Council Annual Report 2001

6

Financial Management

6.1 Intention of the modernisation programme

Expenditure by local authorities in 2000 was €4,665 million (approximately six per cent of GNP). This expenditure is split roughly 50/50 between current and capital expenditure: €2,298 million for day-to-day revenue/current expenditure and €2,367 million for capital expenditure (Dollard, 2003). While expenditure may be low compared with many other European countries, due to the narrower range of functions performed, nevertheless substantial sums of public money are entrusted to local authorities.

In this chapter, the focus is on the development of financial management systems and procedures within local authorities. In this context, Better Local Government (BLG) (1996) notes that the taxpayer needs to be assured that the money allocated to and raised by local authorities is being spent efficiently and effectively, and that there is 'a framework within which the efficiency and value for money agenda will routinely permeate all aspects of financial management'.

The outline of a new financial management system (FMS) for local government is set out in BLG, aimed at giving more transparent information on the real cost of providing services. The main features of the FMS include:

- revising and modernising the existing legal basis underpinning the system
- revising the basis of accounting, including accruals, asset valuation, balance sheets, year end procedures etc
- developing unambiguous accounting standards across all local authorities to allow for standard methods of costing services and for financial reporting purposes
- harmonising the work with that of the Local Government Computer Services Board in the computerisation elements of the new FMS

- rationalising the arrangements for the provision by local authorities of various financial and statistical reports to central government
- reviewing the role of the finance function in local authorities to enable it to provide a strengthened, more professional role in the management of finances within local authority affairs.

Supporting and promoting this move to a new FMS, BLG also sets out an enhanced role for value for money (VFM) concepts and practices, both within local authorities and within the Local Government Audit Service. Similarly, BLG envisages the development of financial performance indicators, with local authorities required to publish each year their performance against these indicators.

Modernising Government notes the progress being made in developing new financial management systems for local authorities and reiterates what are seen as the key elements of the efficiency agenda:

- the strategic decisions made to revamp the local authority accounting system to a full accrual basis
- the development of better and consistent costing of services
- a greater emphasis on value for money, including the internal and external audit systems
- the harnessing of ICT in support of business objectives.

In broad terms, BLG, in describing the aim of the programme of improvement of financial systems states that it will 'enable users of services and local taxpayers to form better judgments as to whether the local authority is delivering an efficient and cost effective service, it will be of considerable benefit to councillors in supporting their role in monitoring performance and in taking a strategic overview of local authority operations. And it will provide individual local authorities with an incentive to match best business practice'.

6.2 The practice

Initial steps to improve financial reporting came with the

production of an accounting code of practice for local authorities, issued in 1998, and the amendment to the abstract of accounts which was renamed the annual financial statement from 1999. As Davis (2003) notes: 'This statement, as well as containing details on actual figures concerning a local authority's revenue (current) account and capital account at year end, also includes a statement of accounting policies, a comparison of performance against budget and notes to the accounts'.

More substantively, these moves have been accompanied by the introduction of the new financial management system (FMS) for local government. The computer package chosen by most local authorities to form the heart of the FMS, Agresso, was piloted in two local authorities and subsequently introduced nationally. FMS is being introduced on a three phase basis. Phase 1, which all local authorities have completed, consisted of the introduction of a general ledger (including fixed assets, stores and bank reconciliation modules) and a purchase ledger. This enables a move from receipt and payment accounting to full accrual accounting with balance sheet. Phase 2 involves the introduction of revenue collection and costing systems, and local authorities are addressing this issue. Phase 3 concerns the active use of Agresso in the whole range of financial decision making across authorities, including the linking of goals and objectives with budgets, management accounting and programme audit.

The process used to implement Agresso seems to have worked well. As well as a national team overseeing the project, each local authority appointed a full time project team. For example, in Dun Laoghaire-Rathdown the project team consisted of a project leader and six 'superusers' responsible for the implementation of the system, with a senior programmer and a systems analyst providing the necessary IT support. The establishment of a project team on its own is not enough, however, and it needs to fit into a broader system of supports, as this quote from an official in North Tipperary County Council in an interview with Byrne (2002) illustrates:

> Well quite a lot of actions occurred, and in my opinion quite successfully to implement Agresso. First of all we set up a project team and incorporated the project team manager onto the management team. We then insisted that all issues related to Agresso be brought up at every management meeting. And then set up a superusers team made up of representatives from areas in the local authority. We also used the IPA to do financial awareness training to a large number of staff including outdoor staff. Finally we employed Mentec to specifically train staff on the hardware and software implications.

While the actual introduction of Agresso has gone well, it has not been an entirely smooth process and several issues have arisen during implementation. Nearly all of the respondents interviewed for this study noted that the introduction of Agresso had been a lot more resource intensive than initially envisaged, and that it was not, initially at least, as user-friendly as had been anticipated. The time taken by project team members has been significant, and the general training needs of staff to help them use the system has been, in the view of many, significantly underestimated. In terms of use of the system, two main issues were highlighted: (a) the use of the system by managers to abstract management information and to improve budget management has been more difficult and progressed slower than anticipated, and (b) at the level of input of data, there have been some difficulties with staff keying in the correct codes and keeping information up-to-date. Data reliability and integrity is a key issue.

It is still early days in terms of changing management responsibility for budgets arising from the introduction of Agresso. In Westmeath, sixty-one budget holders have been designated since spring 2002, with authority and responsibility to manage budgets, within given parameters. This initiative is seen to be working well in its initial stages.

Apart from the introduction of Agresso, there have been other significant developments relating to the FMS. The finance function within local authorities has been significantly upgraded, with the creation of a new more senior post of head of finance replacing the old finance officer post. This move has been complemented by the creation of a financial/management accountant post, to increase the professionalisation of the management of finances within local authorities. At the same time, many local authorities have created or enhanced internal audit units. Among other things, these internal audit units have an important role to play in helping promote a value for money ethos within authorities.

The views of most county and city managers with regard to FMS is that it is too soon as this stage to assess the benefits arising, but that benefits are beginning to flow from the system. Just over half the managers surveyed felt that the quality of financial information available within the authority had increased a lot or very much in recent years.

6.3 *Key issues emerging and suggestions for future developments*

Good progress has been made in the implementation of the financial management computer packages underpinning the FMS and in enhancing the finance function in local authorities. Certainly, compared with the introduction of new financial systems in the civil service under the Management Information Framework (MIF) initiative, progress has been good: the evaluation of the Strategic Management Initiative in the civil service noted that '... the potential benefits of the MIF remain undersold, and the framework does not appear to have captured the attention of many senior managers across the civil service' (PA Consulting Group, 2002a). In contrast, there is a significant degree of senior management engagement with the FMS across local authorities.

In terms of managing the implementation process, the good practice lessons learned from where the introduction of FMS has gone well has implications for other large scale change initiatives. Key success factors include:

- the steering and guidance provided at national level by the national project team

- the quality of the local project teams, including appropriate professional expertise and user involvement
- linkage of the project team work with the management team agenda, thus giving status to the project
- the training support provided, both to enhance specific expertise and to provide background knowledge of the issues concerned.

However, in many ways, the main challenges and potential benefits associated with the implementation of the FMS lie ahead. An updating of the accountancy code is needed to incorporate reporting formats and consistency of presentation. Also, while the basic systems are now in place or are in the process of being put in place, the active use of improved financial information in management decision making and performance improvement initiatives is yet to happen. A significant challenge here is to manage the cultural change involved in moving to more active budgeting. As one interviewee in North Tipperary stated to Byrne (2002):

> You had a system where people ordered goods and looked at the expenditure afterwards when it was too late really because they had already committed against the budget. So they weren't managing their budgets. What they were doing was accounting for their expenditure rather than managing the budget. They were certifying payments after the goods had been received and now what they would be required to do was to approve orders in advance, be responsible and accept responsibility for that ... People have to take responsibility for a budget and there has to be determination of who is a budget holder.

On a similar theme, Horan (2001) notes that although the implementation of an FMS may seem quite simple '... doing it right requires that all managers and staff, not just the finance department, use the system properly. This poses questions in relation to the culture of the authority and the priority attributed to the stewardship and management of finances and budgets'.

Byrne (2002) defines three levels of financial management modernisation, which are set out in Figure 6.1. At level one, there is agreement about the main goals and characteristics of the financial management system, actions are taken to implement financial management modernisation, and problems and limitations are identified and addressed. At level two, decentralisation and widespread participation in the use of financial management systems takes place and the improved information is begun to be used for performance measurement and management control. At level three, line managers are active and responsible budget managers, with the financial management system providing relevant and timely information for decision making, and budgeting

Figure 6.1 Levels of Financial Management Modernisation

Level 1	Level 2	Level 3
1) Main goals 2) Characteristics 3) Actions undertaken 4) Problems and limitations	1) Decentralisation and participation 2) Improve financial management information 3) Enhance management responsibility for performance 4) Performance measurement and spending management control	1) Budget line managers to be key beneficiaries of the reform 2) Relevant and timely decision making 3) Designing and implementing output and performance measurement systems 4) Broaden the scope of reviews and controls 5) Emphasis on the efficiency and effectiveness of spending 6) Coherence of budgeting, management accounting and programme audit 7) Interaction between financial management and general management 8) Change attitudes towards the use of resources 9) Adaptive and participative 10) Management supporting and maintaining change

(Source: Byrne, 2002)

being closely linked to wider management objectives. Using this typology, the FMS in local authorities still has some way to go before the full achievement of level three changes.

It is when the new FMS is integrated into management practice that more effective decisions on costings and the implications of alternative approaches to service delivery will be able to be made. For example, there has been little analysis of the contracting out of services. Yet external review (Reeves and Barrow, 2000) of contracting out of refuse collection services in Ireland notes that tendering can yield savings of between 34 and 45 per cent, with the bulk of these savings attributed to real efficiency gains as a result of contracting out.

The full implementation of the FMS will also require the development of strong accountability and responsibility frameworks. As Horan (2001) indicates:

> Effective accountability frameworks include clarity of roles and responsibilities, agreed performance expectations and mechanisms for monitoring and evaluation in the context of the organisation's annual and medium term plans. This will also incorporate varying degrees of delegation and devolution within each of the main programme areas.

As an illustration of how good financial information can contribute to better decision making, an example from the UK Best Value initiative is informative. Best Value was set up to ensure that councils: challenge why and how services are being provided; compare performance with other local authorities and across the public, voluntary and private sectors; consult with local communities; and embrace fair competition as a means of securing efficient and effective services (Audit Commission, 1999). One of the Best Value pilot initiatives is a benchmarking club entitled CWOIL (from the participating authorities: Cambridge City Council, Welwyn Hatfield Council, Oxford City Council, Ipswich Borough Council and the City of Lincoln). Since 1997, CWOIL has undertaken data benchmarking and key area process mapping in the housing area. Bovaird (2000) describes the process and the outcomes:

- For each service (e.g. repairs, housing advice, waiting list management) a CWOIL service review group was established, with members from each authority, with similar groups established in each authority. The process was co-ordinated by a steering group consisting of all the chief officers from the housing departments. A technical advisors group set protocols for the overall initiative.
- In phase one of the reviews, the authorities agreed detailed definitions of services and costing conventions. They undertook a process analysis, on the basis of which a CWOIL benchmark was drafted, set at the average level of performance reached by the top two of the five authorities. This benchmark was then compared with other housing management agencies and private sector companies and, if appropriate, the benchmark was raised.
- Each authority then consulted with its elected members in order to establish targets upon the benchmarks they had not yet attained.
- The project is seen to be delivering both significant quality improvements and cost savings.

As a further example of international good practice in integrating financial management with service planning, Tilburg City Council in the Netherlands is widely recognised as a leader (indeed, the German reform of local government has been largely inspired by the experience of Tilburg). In Tilburg, the council wanted to move to a system that linked budget inputs and outcomes for service users. The budgeting approach is based on rethinking the work of service units in terms of products (outputs) delivered to customers. Over 230 products have been identified which are categorised into product groups and policy areas. Product descriptions distinguish between the activities carried out, the product that they lead to and outcome targets. These elements are defined and measured annually. Costs are assigned to products and the budget is constructed on this basis (Pekdemir, 1995; Audit Commission, 1999). As a result, councillors and managers have better information on costs and performance for decision making and citizens are better informed about how money is spent and the performance of services.

These international examples indicate that, while financial management systems and procedures have improved significantly in Ireland, there is still some way to go in terms of using the new FMS to full effect. It is important that the progress made to date is seen as the first step on the way toward a more integrated system of service and financial planning and management.

7

Human Resource Management

7.1 Intention of the modernisation programme

In late 2001, the Local Government Management Services Board (LGMSB), itself a product of *Better Local Government* (BLG) (1996), commissioned a comprehensive review of the HR function in local government (PA Consulting Group, 2002b). The purpose of this chapter is not to replicate that exercise, which presents a long-term view of reform of the HR function in local authorities. Rather, as with the other chapters in this report, the intention is to review progress in respect of the change agenda set out in BLG. However, where appropriate, the findings of the PA Consulting Group report are referred to.

Just over 30,000 people are employed in the local government sector in Ireland. While acknowledging some positive features of the local authority personnel system, for example open recruitment for senior positions, BLG describes it as a critical area for reform. In particular, the need to:

- devolve decisions in respect of HRM to local authority management teams
- create a new management tier, with responsibility for developing more strategic thinking in relation to the authorities' programmes
- establish more professional HR units
- develop partnership
- enhance the availability of flexible work arrangements
- review the recruitment process to better reflect modern conditions and needs
- significantly improve staff development programmes
- ensure a higher proportion of women at management level

- ensure that the number of people with disabilities employed is at least 3 per-cent.

Since 1996 a number of other policy and legislative initiatives have either enabled or further promoted the reform agenda outlined in BLG. *Modernising Government* (2000) emphasised the importance of introducing 'a management structure based on performance, with clear lines of delegation of authority, responsibility and accountability'. This was followed, in 2001, by the Local Government Act. One of the key features of this legislation is that it reduces the role of the Minister for Environment and Local Government in respect of local authority personnel matters (Sections 155-165). Staffing, remuneration and conditions of employment are, subject to a number of conditions, matters for individual authorities. The Act also removes the distinction between officers and non-officers in local authorities.

The *Programme for Prosperity and Fairness* (PPF) (2000) further maps out objectives with respect to HR modernisation in the public sector. In particular, in local government the need to:

- strengthen management and staffing structures
- implement a range of HR strategies with particular emphasis on the training and development function
- eliminate obstacles to flexibility and efficiency such as the dual structure
- further develop partnership structures introduced under *Partnership 2000*.

Most local authority corporate plans were drafted around the same time as the publication of PPF, in late 2000, and so do not fully represent the obligations contained in the section on modernisation in the local government sector. It is therefore important that operational plans, which are required under PPF to deliver the content of the corporate plans, reflect these developments.

Finally, following on from the production of corporate and operational plans, PPF describes the next step in local government modernisation as the development and implementation of a performance management system to ensure effective implementation of objectives contained in the plans. Performance management in the context of local authorities is described as encompassing:

- performance planning
- ongoing management of performance
- annual performance and development review.

Since PPF this has been broadened to also include the performance and development of individual staff members. A sector wide performance management advisory and monitoring group has been established under the auspices of the LGMSB and given responsibility for the implementation of performance management. In late 2002, this group commissioned a scoping report to explore how a performance management system might take account of the complex environment of the local authority sector and be flexible enough to reflect the varying requirements and culture of individual local authorities. The scoping report is to be followed by design and implementation phases.

7.2 The practice

This section considers current HR practice in local authorities under several headings. However, firstly, it is relevant to note the key findings of the PA Consulting Group (2002b) *Review of the Human Resource Function in Local Authorities*. While the consultants found evidence of some good HR practice in local authorities, based on survey and interview evidence they conclude that:

- there is little evidence of a strategic approach to HR
- there is little evidence that HR is considered an integral responsibility of senior line managers
- current HR practice continues to exhibit a strong adherence to inherited or traditional personnel administration procedures
- considerable ambiguity surrounds the proper location and ownership of HR within the local authority system.

There were, therefore, significant limitations in HR practice. These limitations, and examples of good practice aimed at addressing them, are examined below for particular activities: the implementation of new staffing structures; the professionalisation of HR in local authorities; how HR is addressed in corporate plans; devolution of responsibility from the DELG; and partnership.

7.2.1 The implementation of new staffing structures

One of the most significant changes proposed by BLG is reform of local government management structures. The objective is to create a new management tier with clear responsibility for the adoption of a more strategic approach to the delivery of local authority programmes. The new positions are also seen as facilitating the break down of the dual structure, whereby professional and administrative staff in local authorities had separate career paths, through the abolition of the city/county engineer post and the introduction of the new generalist director of service positions.

In a majority of councils, directors of service positions were only filled during the first half of 2002. The delay in implementing the staffing reforms recommended in BLG was due to ongoing union/management negotiations. In particular, the unions were concerned at what they saw as a lack of consultation at the design stage and, as a result, negotiations in relation to the implementation of the new structures were far more protracted than might otherwise have been the case. Also, the unions view was that outdoor staff in particular were not sufficiently considered in the planned changes.

While it is too early to comment conclusively on the impact of the reformed structure, a number of variations and trends are evident. Firstly, while the majority of councils have appointed directors of service with responsibility for a particular function (e.g. housing) or a range of functions (e.g. corporate affairs and HRM), in a small number of cases (e.g. Donegal) directors have also been given area responsibilities. In general, the findings of the survey of city and county managers, undertaken as part of this research, suggest that the new structures are contributing to the adoption of a more strategic and corporate approach to the delivery of services within local authorities as Table 7.1 illustrates. Furthermore, concerns among senior engineers that they would lose out to staff with a generalist background in the filling of the director of service positions have, overall, not been realised.

Table 7.1 County and city managers' views on new management structures

	Not at all	A little	A fair amount	A lot	Very much	Total
The introduction of a new management structure has resulted in a more strategic approach to the delivery of services within the authority	0%	7%	28%	48%	17%	100%

Donegal County Council has taken a particularly systematic approach to the development of new management and organisational structures. Changes were made in consultation with staff using the partnership process, with direction being given by a project team established by the county manager, and supported by an organisational specialist. Within each of seven functional areas under directors of service, four levels have been established: three levels of management (director, divisional manager and area manager) together with the front line staffing grades. Roles, responsibilities and accountabilities have been clarified for all levels from the county manager down (see Donegal County Council, 2002 for details). This approach is influenced by the organisations design theories of Jaques (1997).

However, more generally across authorities, a number of issues have arisen as a result of the restructuring at middle management level (senior executive officers) and below. One issue is the sheer scale of change involved. One county manager noted that within the council, 70 per cent of staff have new roles since the reformed structures were put in place in September 2001. This huge change reflects the adaptability and commitment of staff. But in some instances it appears that the restructuring process, and the consequent creation of vacancies at all levels, raised considerable expectations of promotion opportunities that were not always realised, leading in some instances to industrial relations difficulties. In addition, a major objective for restructuring was to improve management at all levels in local authorities. However, it appears that some individuals have been promoted primarily on the basis of technical competence and lack the skills or experience to enable them to effectively adopt the management aspects of their new position. Finally, there appears to be some transitional difficulties in some cases as a result of the changed reporting structures, for example engineers adapting to no longer necessarily reporting to a senior professional but rather to the head of the function.

Training and development is an urgent requirement in this regard and is actively being explored by the LGMSB who during 2001 commissioned training needs analyses of both managers in the local government sector (PricewaterhouseCoopers, 2002) and other local authority staff (Institute of Public Administration, 2002). The reports prioritise the training needs of staff taking on leadership roles, in particular emphasising the need for managers to develop and enhance performance management, staff development, team-work, staff communications and decision making skills.

7.2.2 The professionalisation of HR in local authorities

The growing importance of HRM within local authorities is reflected in the increasing size and status of HR units. Traditionally, local authority personnel offices had a small number of staff and were responsible for the administrative side of personnel. However, the increasing recognition of the role HRM plays in meeting business objectives, and the consequent need for individual authorities to have greater autonomy in respect of HR decisions, has resulted in rapid change in this regard.

With the introduction of the director of service positions, typically, though not in all cases, HRM has become the responsibility of the Director for Corporate Affairs. In addition a new senior officer position has been created, with day-to-day responsibility for the HR function. The number of other staff in the unit has also increased, in some cases with officers being given specific responsibility for areas like training and development or industrial relations.

The expanded role of HR units, for example the necessity to review contracts and role profiles following the changes brought about by BLG, together with the necessity to develop policy in relation to a range of strategic issues, such as performance management, career progression and manpower planning, has resulted in the need for HR units to devolve responsibility in respect of staff management issues to line managers. However, it is also recognised that this development is in itself desirable and efforts are being made within local authorities to encourage line managers, who are responsible for the output of a unit, to have greater input into the selection and management of staff working for them. County and city managers feel, by and large, that there is still some way to go in involving line managers in the active management of their staff.

In Limerick City Council, where concerns have been expressed in relation to devolution of responsibility for personnel issues to line managers, it has served to highlight the urgent need for a comprehensive HR strategy. The strategy will set out policies and procedures to reflect changed HR requirements and outline the council's commitment in relation to performance management and ongoing staff development. It is also seen as an opportunity to highlight to staff the standards required in respect of performance and delivery and requirements in relation to devolution of responsibility for staff management issues to line managers.

7.2.3 How HR is addressed in corporate plans

All local authorities address HR/personnel/staff issues in their corporate plans, either under the general heading of corporate services or in a dedicated section. There is an effort in the majority of plans to articulate overarching objectives in relation to HR. Typically, this relates to the value placed on its employees and the fact that priority will be given to their development and welfare. In a small number of cases more detailed breakdowns of objectives are made. For example, Kerry County Council details seven goals of HRM, including the need to ensure employees have the skills necessary to enable them to fulfil their role and develop their careers and the need to promote a culture of equality of opportunity in the organisation.

While there is some variation in the terminology used, the majority of plans treat the elaboration of objectives in a broadly similar way, with reference being made to strategies, actions and targets that are intended to support the achievement of HR objectives. Strategies vary in number from three to twenty, with the dominant themes being the need to conduct training needs analyses followed by the implementation of a staff training and development programme, the preparation of staff welfare guides or the introduction of employee assistance programmes and actions in relation to heath and safety. However, a broad range of other HR related issues are also included on strategy lists, for example more effective recruitment procedures, IT arrangements and training for staff, the development of induction and mobility policies, the introduction of flexible work arrangements, the promotion of equality, internal communications, staff suggestion schemes and partnership. Overall, the general criticism made in Chapter 6, that objectives and strategies tend to be over general and ambiguous, holds true in relation to the sections on HR.

Only a small number of plans refer to the development of HR strategies that will set out objectives for the management and development of HRM in the authority as a priority (e.g. Limerick City, Monaghan, Offaly, Waterford County). Similarly, only a minority of plans include references to performance management. In the case of Dun Laoghaire-Rathdown County Council, the relevant action point is to 'provide opportunities for staff to discuss their role with their supervisors on a regular basis', whereas others refer to the introduction of a specific scheme. Limerick City in particular gives priority to this area, including the development and implementation of a performance management system as a high level objective with a range of related specific strategies.

7.2.4 Devolution of responsibility from the Department of the Environment and Local Government

BLG notes that, traditionally within local government, standardisation has been achieved 'through considerable central involvement and an extensive array of statutory consent procedures operated by the Department of the Environment and Local Government (DELG) relating to pay, numbers, conditions of service, qualifications for appointments, recruitment procedures and so forth'. However, it is argued that these controls can have a dampening effect on local management initiative and lead to a culture of referral to central government. As a result, a process of devolvement of responsibility for HR matters from the DELG was instigated subject to budgetary constraints. This initiative was given statutory support under the Local Government Act, 2001.

In practice devolution has been slow to impact on local authorities. For example, it would appear that authorities are only slowly introducing grievance and disciplinary procedures and raising awareness among line managers of the importance of maintaining appropriate records and adhering to best practice in relevant cases. In this regard, the role of the LGMSB, in providing a support system for local authorities in relation to HR matters and providing guidance in the design and implementation of appropriate procedures, is significant.

However, for individual local authorities seeking to be pro-active and develop policies in relation to issues outside of the BLG agenda, or to proceed at a faster pace than that of the sector in general, there is still a requirement to consult with the DELG, which remains concerned that local authorities 'act collectively in certain aspects of their human resource policies to ensure consistency (BLG)'. This constraint appears in particular to affect larger authorities, with well-established HR units and the resources and experiences to move forward unilaterally in relation to HR modernisation. However, while this can be a cause of some frustration, there also appears to be an understanding that all authorities are part of the local government sector and must work in tandem, both with other local authorities and the LGMSB, to promote reform across the sector.

7.2.5 Partnership

A central component of the *Partnership 2000* (1996) national agreement was the importance of replacing an adversarial approach to change with one based on effective consultation and participation. Within the local authority sector this led to discussions at national level in relation to the introduction of workplace partnership and the establishment of a national advisory group for partnership involving both management and union representatives.

The role of the Local Authority National Partnership Advisory Group (LANPAG) is to support the partnership process within the local government sector and to provide a national level forum within which to assist the advancement of partnership at local level. In this capacity, the first task of the LANPAG was to develop a framework for the implementation of partnership in local authorities. This led to the establishment, by 2001, of joint management, union and staff partnership committees in all the thirty-four city and county councils. Initial partnership training was provided to participants in relation to the goals of national partnership, the role of local authority committees and how to function as an effective team. National funding also enabled the appointment of partnership facilitators to assist in the development of workplace partnership through the provision of operational, administrative and training support to committees.

There is widespread acknowledgment of the potential for partnership committees to play an important role in implementing change in local authorities. However, the level of activity of committees and the degree to which they have become established varies throughout the country. The views of county and city managers on partnership are illustrated in Table 7.2. The general approach adopted by committees has been to establish working groups to address specific issues. In most instances, with the

Table 7.2 County and city managers' views on partnership

	Not at all	A little	A fair amount	A lot	Very much	Total
Partnership has helped to develop/resolve initiatives that would not have been introduced/resolved otherwise	0%	24%	48%	14%	14%	100%

assistance of the partnership facilitators, committees have been able to identify a broad number of potential work areas and have had considerable success in tackling projects in relation to areas such as health and safety, office accommodation, employment policies, the development of staff handbooks and training and development. However, in a number of cases the challenge of getting engagement from the bottom up has proven more difficult, with management having to suggest issues for the committee to look at.

The majority of partnership activity has been focused on relatively self-contained non-contentious issues. This is understandable given the importance, noted in the review of partnership in local authorities (Lazes, 2002), of achieving several 'breakthrough' projects to encourage motivation and commitment within committees. However, two councils where partnership committees have successfully addressed projects with significant industrial relations implications are Limerick City and Dublin City. In Limerick the best practice guidelines in relation to the 'Future Structure and Organisation of the Housing Maintenance Department', agreed through a partnership working group, included the closing of some depots, the opening of a new depot and the reorganisation of breaks (Limerick City Council Partnership Committee, 2001). In Dublin, the structured reduction of car parking spaces available to staff, in line with the council's public transport and traffic strategies for the city, was facilitated by the workings of the partnership committee.

7.3 *Key issues emerging and suggestions for future developments*

BLG sets out an extensive agenda in respect of reform of HRM in local government. The devolution of decisions in respect of human resource issues to individual authorities, the strengthening of management structures, the professionalisation of personnel units and the introduction of performance management are all central to the overall modernisation process. In this context, many county and city managers stressed that HR reform was still very much at an early stage, and that a significant amount of work is still needed.

Strategies in relation to the implementation of this agenda should in principle be set out in corporate plans. This will be a key challenge for the next iteration of corporate plans. In the meantime, but also to assist in determining priorities, an urgent task for HR units is the development, required under PPF, of annual operational plans. Specific targets in respect of objectives, activities and related performance indicators should also be included.

In relation to some aspects of the reform agenda, for example the restructuring of management and the elimination of the dual structure, significant change has been implemented over a short period of time. While it appears that staffing reforms have led to a more strategic approach to the delivery of services, concerns remain in relation to the lack of management skills and expertise of some newly promoted staff, particularly at middle management level. There is also a widespread view that outdoor staff should be given more attention from a HR perspective. More generally, it is interesting to note the variations in how local authorities are applying the new structures. It could be useful to review this diverse experience and assess lessons learned.

As a sector, local government appears to be grappling with the issue of devolution: both the increased autonomy individual authorities have in respect of staff relations' issues and also internally from the HR unit to line managers. These changes have been particularly challenging to implement, because line managers have been slow to accept a situation whereby the personnel unit's role in respect of staff management issues might evolve towards one primarily of guidance.

A further consequence of the professionalisation of the HR function within local authorities is that it suggests an increasing need for specialist training and skills for staff working in this area. However, the implication of this is that local authorities should move away from the traditional approach, whereby all staff are regarded as generalists capable of adapting to work in any area, to one where increasing specialisation is required. There is as yet no general consensus on the merits of specialisation versus generalist skills or the appropriate balance between them.

The development of a system of performance management and the implementation of training and development programmes are important requirements in assisting local authorities to overcome some of the challenges occasioned by new staffing structures and the professionalisation of HR. However, in order for reforms to become embedded, there is also a need for change in attitudes and cultures, for example, in relation to amended reporting structures and the importance of managers accepting responsibility for staff relations' issues.

Inevitably cultural change can only happen over a period of time. However, greater acceptance of a new approach to HRM in local authorities might be facilitated by presenting reform in this regard not simply as devolution, which might be construed by some as the abdication by HR units of all responsibility in respect of staff management issues, but rather to emphasise what is in fact the reality in this regard – the development of a strategic partnership between HR units and managers. This is the approach that is being taken, for example, in Dublin City Council.

One of the more successful aspects of local government reform has been the implementation of partnership in local authorities. The review carried out on behalf of LANPAG notes that the partnership process has lead to greater access to information, improved consultation and enhanced opportunities for staff to participate in decision making.

However, these benefits relate primarily to the partnership process and, as highlighted in the Lazes (2002) review, the challenge in moving forward is to emphasise outcomes, and in particular the importance of setting clear, measurable goals. Several county and city managers noted that, while partnership has been good at addressing some of the 'softer' issues, it is time now to also focus on some of the more difficult and intransigent issues.

Overall, it would appear that there needs to be a greater recognition, within the local government sector, that aspects of the HR reform agenda cannot happen in isolation of each other. Reform has to take place on several fronts simultaneously. For example, challenges occasioned by the implementation of new staffing structures point to the urgent need for the implementation of performance management and training and development programmes. In this regard, the role of the LGMSB is significant, as an organisation dedicated to the provision of a comprehensive support system for the human resource function in local authorities.

Part 4

Quality Services

8

Customer Action Plans and Service Indicators

8.1 Intention of the modernisation programme

The achievement of a significant and on-going improvement in the delivery of services to the public is a key objective of the public service modernisation programme at local government level (see Humphreys, Fleming and O'Donnell 1999). One of the cornerstones of this approach has been the requirement for local authorities to publish customer action plans (CAPs) setting out the action they intend to take to achieve tangible improvements in the quality of public services they deliver. The initial impetus behind the production of CAPs in the local government sector can be traced back to *Better Local Government* (BLG) (1996):

> Ireland needs and deserves a public service which operates to the highest standards, both in the quality of its decision making and in the quality of service provided at the point of impact on the customer ... in the public service, there is the danger that insufficient attention may be paid to the needs of the customer and that internal demands, preferences and perceptions of the organisation may take precedence. To counteract this, there is a need to establish systems to ensure that those responsible for the delivery of services are driven by the requirements of customer needs and customer satisfaction and that services are viewed from the customers', rather than the organisations', perspective. In this way, government is made more responsive and the customer better served.

The PPF (2000) further required public service bodies to develop and implement challenging customer service standards in consultation with the customer. It is against this policy backdrop that the development of CAPs in the local government sector as an integral part of the corporate planning process came about. *Modernising Government*

(2000) recognised that 'the primary impetus must come from within organisations themselves. This will require an ongoing focus on customers' needs and requirements, informed by internal and external consultation. Customer service plans can then be developed and implemented as part of the SMI process. These plans can identify customer service objectives along with the levels and standards of service which customers can reasonably expect. They should be developed and articulated in the corporate plans'. A commitment is also given by the DELG that it would 'as far as possible respond positively to requests to assist in the funding of customer service initiatives'.

The impetus within local authorities for the adoption of a CAP approach to promoting customer services also derives from national developments under the quality customer service (QCS) initiative since 1997 (see Humphreys, 1998). Initially focusing upon the services provided by government departments/offices, but widened out to the broader public service (including local government in July 2000) as a result of government decision, this nation-wide initiative seeks to promote the adoption of improved customer service standards. To facilitate this process, public service organisations are required to produce a two-year customer action plan indicating how full effect would be given to the guiding principles for the delivery of quality customer service. These twelve guiding principles (set out in full in Appendix 5) are: quality standards; equality/diversity; physical access; information; timeliness and courtesy; complaints; appeals; consultation and evaluation; choice; official languages equality; better co-ordination; and internal customer.

With regard to service indicators, under BLG (1996), local authorities are asked to set standards in respect of a number of indicators and to measure progress in relation to agreed standards. BLG also proposes that these service delivery indicators be combined with financial performance indicators to produce a comprehensive picture of performance. In a similar vein, PPF (2000) notes the development of performance measurement and performance management as part of the modernisation programme in the local government sector.

In May 2000 the DELG issued a note on the development of service indicators in local authorities (Department of the Environment and Local Government, 2000). The minister, in consultation with local authorities, drew up a set of service indicators to apply to all local authorities. Authorities are required to measure their performance against the indicators and publish the results in their annual reports. The intention is to '... allow local councillors and the public to judge how their council is performing by comparison with other similar councils and it will be a spur to council managements to step up performance' (DELG, 2000). Details of the service indicators chosen are given in Appendix 6.

In summary, the modernisation process in local government aims at encouraging the more widespread and effective use of customer action plans and performance indicators in order to improve the quality of service delivery. The intention is to promote a more systematic and structured approach to quality of service issues, particularly in the light of strategies and targets set out in corporate and operational plans.

8.2 The practice

In assessing the current series of customer action plans and service indicators produced by local authorities it is important to acknowledge that 'no one size fits all'. As BLG (1996) stressed: 'it is a matter for local authorities to develop their own quality initiatives in accordance with local circumstances and priorities and to set out their intentions in this regard in their SMI strategy statements (corporate plans) – different approaches can be adopted to similar issues'. However, while mindful of the desirability of local flexibility in responding to local circumstance, it is also important to assess the extent to which the current series of CAPs as a whole have responded positively to the type of approach proposed in *Modernising Government* (2000), namely that local authority customer action plans (CAPs) should:

- build upon internal and external consultation
- identify QCS objectives
- specify levels and standards of service and
- place the CAP within the wider context of the authority's corporate plan.

Furthermore, it is important to review and assess the extent and manner in which local government is addressing the twelve guiding principles for quality customer service. The review of CAP and service indicator practice presented below draws upon views expressed by key informants during the course of this study, the specific feedback received from the questionnaire survey of county and city managers, as well as a detailed content analysis of all current plans and annual reports. The review is also informed by previous work in the area of QCS and performance indicators undertaken by the Committee for Public Management Research as well as an assessment of civil service CAPs undertaken by Butler (2002).

8.2.1 An overview of the CAPs

The results from the questionnaire survey of county and city managers clearly indicate that all respondents felt the introduction of a CAP in their authority had given a 'clear focus to quality service delivery issues' (see Table 8.1). While the range of services provided by Irish local authorities is comparatively limited by international standards (see Chapter 2), the 2000 and 2001 annual reports of the Office of the Ombudsman have recently highlighted shortcomings in the quality of some services provided, e.g. regarding the operation of the planning system. Remedial action is being taken to improve this situation but there is little doubt that CAPs can also play an important role in helping to raise standards on an authority-wide basis. As such they have considerable potential to act as valuable tools for change and it will be important to learn from the experiences gained from developing and implementing this first series of plans.

Table 8.1 County and city managers' views on customer action plans

	Not at all	A little	A fair amount	A lot	Very much	Total
The Customer Action Plan has given a clearer focus to quality service delivery issues	0%	3%	24%	59%	14%	100%

For example, in reading all the CAPs, together with their associated corporate plans, it is clear that the vast majority of authorities have embarked upon hitherto uncharted waters in preparing their first CAP. That, of course, does not mean to imply that local government as a whole, as well as individual local authorities, have not been active for many years in seeking to improve the quality of services they provide. However, it is clear that for the vast majority of local authorities there is a variety in content, quality and approach that suggests the need for greater central guidance and support. There is also a need for improved opportunities for those with lead responsibility for the production of such plans to be able to network with each other to share good practice and to share experiences in addressing problems and challenges that arise. Such experiences are very similar to those experienced at central government level following the initial introduction of CAPs there in 1997.

It is also evident that the varied appearance and content of the current series of plans suggests a degree of uncertainty and divergence of opinion as to the purpose of these documents. The original guidance for the production of CAPs at local government level envisaged their integration within the authorities' corporate plans, possibly as inserts that could be readily distributed to the public. In practice, the CAP element within the larger body of the corporate plan is often comparatively small. Occasionally, little more has been done than to reprint the twelve guiding principles of quality customer service, without indicating the specific measures being taken by the authority to operationalise these principles in business processes.

A number of local authorities have produced stand alone CAP documents which are more amenable to independent and wider distribution to citizens/customers through council offices, local libraries etc. Such authorities include Clare, Carlow, Cavan, Dublin City, Dun Laoghaire-Rathdown, Laois, Leitrim, Limerick City, Mayo, Meath, North Tipperary, Offaly, Roscommon, South Tipperary, Westmeath and Wexford.

While acknowledging that important issues remain to be resolved regarding access to e-government based services (see Timonen, O'Donnell and Humphreys, 2003), and regardless of whether the CAP is stand alone or not, there is presently only limited and variable use of the Internet by local authorities for the pro-active dissemination of information on their commitments under QCS. Likewise, little information is provided on the dissemination strategies adopted more widely by local authorities to raise awareness of, and promote engagement with, their CAPs.

8.2.2 Response to the twelve guiding principles

In examining the content of the CAPs overall, a number of very positive common features can be identified. For example, most but by no means all plans contain important information on the names and areas of responsibility of key council staff as well as the names and electoral areas of elected representatives. Good practice examples include detailed directories of service, including office/staff contact details (i.e. telephone numbers and/or email addresses), as well as opening hours. CAPs containing several such features include, Carlow, Clare, Dun Laoghaire-Rathdown, Kildare, Kerry, Leitrim, Limerick City, Offaly, Roscommon, South Dublin, North Tipperary, Tipperary South and Westmeath.

Most of the CAPs contain, for the first time, published service standards of varying specificity across the range of services provided. Such openness and accountability is well in advance of that provided by most government departments/offices in the second wave of their CAPs and should be noted as an example of good practice. In a number of cases, local authorities have expressed their commitment to improved service standards within the context of a 'customer charter', which can be a valuable but not essential means of expressing an authority's commitment to its citizens/customers. Examples include Carlow, Dublin City, Dun Laoghaire-Rathdown, Fingal, Mayo, South Dublin and Wicklow. In addition, whether expressed in the form of a charter or not, a number of authorities balance their commitments to the citizen/customer by indicating what the authority may need in return in order to provide a quality service. Authorities such as Kerry, Limerick City, Limerick County, Mayo and Meath explicitly include sections in their CAPs entitled, 'Help us to help you'.

It is evident from many of the CAPs that local authorities have either begun to put in train, or have concrete plans to introduce, more open and transparent complaints and appeals handling arrangements. This is an area that has been subject to criticism from the Office of the Ombudsman in the past. It is timely that engagement with the QCS initiative is providing an overall framework within which improved complaints/appeals procedures can go hand in hand with efforts to raise service standards and improve the quality of information available to citizens/customers. For example, the Dun Laoghaire-Rathdown CAP includes considerable detail on such a scheme. Similarly, efforts are also evident in some CAPs to address the issue of choice in the delivery of services, e.g. by improving access hours and the availability of services on line.

Likewise, often as part of wider social inclusion strategies, it is encouraging to note efforts being made by some local authorities to improve physical access to council services and adopt a pro-active review of current policies and procedures to ensure improved responsiveness in service provision equality and diversity terms. In these latter areas, however, evidence of informed action is comparatively limited and there would appear to be considerable scope for enhanced support to local authorities through the provision of expert advice and guidance from appropriate statutory bodies, such as the Equality Authority (EA) and the National Disability Authority (NDA). Such support is already available to an extent, e.g. in *Ask me: Guidelines for Effective Consultation with People with Disabilities* (NDA, 2002) and the *Support Pack on the Equality/Diversity Aspects of Quality Customer Service for the Civil and Public Service* (Department of the Taoiseach and EA, 2001). Perhaps the least developed area of all in the current series of CAPs relates to official languages equality. While most plans include minimal use of the Irish language and make general commitments to the provision of quality services through the medium of Irish, only three plans are genuinely bilingual – Galway, Kerry and Limerick County.

Progress in relation to effective and developing internal consultation is limited in the CAPs but, in the light of newly available good practice guidance, is likely to improve further over time (see Humphreys, 2002 and O'Riordan and Humphreys, 2003). Especially through the use of partnership committees and providing evidence of consequential strategies to support staff in the delivery of quality services, there is clear commitment in a number of plans to effective engagement with the internal customer in the development and delivery of services. The Longford CAP, for example, contains details of efforts the authority is making in this area to address internal communication and training needs.

There is evidence in a large number of plans of a range of external consultation arrangements in the development and/or delivery of the plans. A number of authorities have commissioned independent external surveys of their customer base, e.g. Kildare, Wicklow and Waterford County. In Waterford County, they have followed up on the survey by developing operational action plans in individual departments to address issues raised in the survey. This represents a good example of ensuring systematic and practical follow-on from customer surveys, often a missing link in the process

A larger number of authorities have also used customer

surveys to gauge opinion in relation to specific service areas, e.g. motor taxation. Even more innovatively, a number of authorities either have and/or are considering customer panels to assist in the on-going development of services (for example, Dublin City and South Dublin County Council). Finally, the issue of better co-ordination and service integration is covered in Chapter 9.

8.2.3 An overview of service indicators

Most authorities are complying with the requirement to report performance against service indicators in their annual reports. The style of this reporting varies. Some local authorities have a separate section listing the service indicators together in one section of the report. In other authorities, the service indicators are spread out and reported on in the section of the report dealing with particular service programmes such as housing and roads. In this latter case, the service indicators are often mixed with other indicators and can be difficult to find at times.

County and city managers surveyed as part of this research still regard it as very much early days in the development and use of service indicators. Approximately two-thirds of managers surveyed stated that service indicators are only used a little or a fair amount to monitor the delivery of quality services (see Table 8.2). Several managers indicated that procedures for gathering information in respect of service indicators are still being developed.

Table 8.2 County and city managers' views of service indicators

	Not at all	A little	A fair amount	A lot	Very much	Total
Service indicators are actively used to monitor our delivery of quality services	0%	21%	45%	24%	10%	100%

Also in terms of reporting on service indicators in the annual report, most authorities simply report their performance against the service indicator for the year under scrutiny: there is no comparative data either over time, against standards or in comparison with other authorities. One notable exception here is Kerry, where in the 2000 annual report different benchmarks are used to plot performance in some service programmes. In the case of the refusal rate for planning permission, for example, the percentage refusal rate in Kerry is shown over a five year period and also in comparison with the national average for rural counties.

8.3 *Key issues emerging and suggestions for future developments*

Gaster (1995) identifies a number of key stages in the service quality improvement process. A public service body needs to:

- identify and involve key interests or stakeholders
- develop explicit organisational values and objectives
- develop ideal (long-term) and attainable (medium-term) service standards
- identify service gaps, strengths and weaknesses
- identify options for future action
- implement a programme of change, and then
- monitor and review those changes.

The promotion and adoption of customer actions plans by local authorities has provided a valuable, introductory planning framework within which each of these key stages can be successfully tackled. The above review indicates that in areas such as improved information provision, the specification of service standards and indicators and commitment to introduce/improve complaint/appeal handling systems, this opportunity for planned improvement is being grasped by a number of local authorities across the country. Further efforts are needed, however, in many of the local authorities to drive forward quality improvements in respect of the twelve guiding principles.

Likewise, while some plans clearly demonstrate that they have been produced via a process of effective internal and external stakeholder consultation, such plans are in a minority. Similarly, while it is evident that some authorities have taken considerable care in both their preparation and presentation of their CAPs, with a demonstrated commitment to delivery, evaluation and substantive change, other plans are skeletal in content and superficial in their approach. Improved usage of central level guidance and support, combined with healthy inter-authority competition, co-operation and peer review, should help in improving both the quality and content of the next generation of CAPs.

In some plans, there is evidence that local authorities are engaging seriously with the significant challenges that arise when seeking to use CAPs as part of a wider strategy to mainstream customer service values more effectively. Mainstreaming a customer service ethos and approach within an organisation can pose searching questions for existing management and work practices. Indeed, the whole-hearted adoption of customer service values often requires nothing short of a fundamental reorientation of that organisation and a radical change in its prevailing culture. Similarly, effective use of a partnership approach to promote QCS within local authorities can assist in spreading ownership of, and a commitment to, customer-focused change. Indeed, excellence in service delivery is best approached as part of an overall drive for quality within a local authority and should not be treated in isolation from other key dimensions, like investment in its people and the development of leadership. In this regard, engagement with external quality frameworks, such as the EU-wide Common Assessment Framework (CAF), can provide a valuable diagnostic tool, help promote joined-up quality focused thinking in the organisation, as well as providing the opportunity for constructive benchmarking. The whole purpose of adopting a quality approach to the delivery of public services is to achieve tangible improvements in standards. Only in a few years' time will it be possible to assess the value of CAPs in helping move local authorities forward.

Similarly, with regard to service indicators it is likely to be some time before it is possible to assess their contribution to improving the quality of service provided by local authorities. However, it is still useful to review experience to date and assess the degree to which the service indicators are being found useful in practice, or if the indicator set should be developed or changed in the light of experience. Certainly there is scope for more use to bc made of comparative benchmarking of performance by authorities, either over time, against standards or with selected groupings of other authorities. This issue has been noted in previous work for the Committee for Public Management Research (Boyle, 2000). As things stand at present there is little evidence of councillors and the public judging how their council is performing in a comparative context, as intended when service indicators were introduced.

It could also be useful, in building on the service indicators experience, to engage more actively with local citizens in the development and use of such indicators. The litter survey conducted annually by An Taisce on behalf of the Irish Business Against Litter Group represents an example of developing outcome-focused indicators of interest to the general public. An interesting case study is Iowa (USA) where, nine municipal governments have begun to implement a model of citizen-initiated performance assessment (Ho and Coates, 2002). Here, a citizen performance team is founded, comprising councillors, administrators and citizen representatives. As illustrated in Figure 8.1, this team develops performance indicators based on a citizen view of important outcomes, collects the data, and disseminates the information to the public. There is thus an active engagement with the public in the development and use of service indicators.

Figure 8.1 The Iowa Citizen-Initiated Performance Assessment Framework

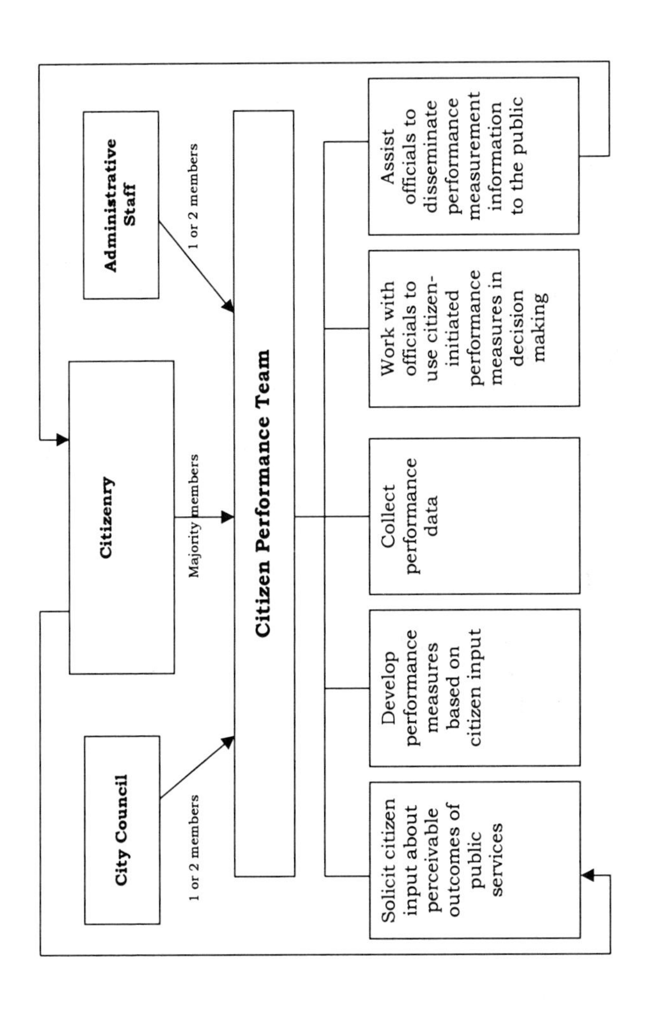

(Source: Ho and Coates, 2002)

9

One-stop-shops/Integrated Service Delivery

9.1 Intention of the modernisation programme

One of the key aims of the local government modernisation process is to develop an efficient and well-managed local government system organised on a customer-focused basis. The delivery of services through one-stop-shops, or integrated service centres, is one of the central elements of more customer-focused service provision. The one-stop-shop concept was brought onto the local government modernisation agenda through *Better Local Government* (BLG) (1996). In more general terms, it could also be said that the integrated service delivery model is part of the broader thinking on decentralisation.

One-stop-shop/integrated service delivery initiatives have sought to fundamentally change the way in which public services are delivered to citizens. The idea behind one-stop-shop projects is a new, customer-oriented view of how services should be organised and delivered. In the traditional public service model, services are organised around bureaucratic structures, and delivered by a large number of unconnected offices that are designed first and foremost for the convenience of service providers, not service users. In contrast, the main idea behind one-stop centres is to organise services according to the needs of customers. This is done through a single contact point that acts as a gateway to a number of services, thus making 'office-hopping' unnecessary: '[t]he essence of the concept relates to the provision of a number of public services on a co-ordinated basis, in a particular location and according to the needs of the customer' (DELG, March 1997).

Apart from this very general definition, there is no set form for a one-stop-shop. For instance, the selection of services offered differs between one-stop centres, as does the level of service offered. At the most basic level, only information and advice are offered, and at the most advanced level applications are received and processed, and decisions/grants/licences requested are issued by the one-stop-shop. However, 'ideally there should be a single contact point where people can get information and advice on the full range of public services, submit claims or applications for such services, and receive the services required' (DELG, 1997).

Local authorities are well placed to seize the opportunity in relation to one-stop-shop centres, due to their multi-purpose remit and wide geographical coverage. Moreover, it was expected that one-stop-shop initiatives would be further aided by the fact that local authority headquarters are increasingly organised on the one-stop-shop principle, and by the fact that local authority libraries are already used to disseminate information about a range of public services.

9.2 *The practice*

The one-stop-shop project started when the DELG sent out a circular to all local authority managers in 1997 launching a pilot programme of one-stop-shops. On the basis of the applications received, five pilot projects were selected in 1998. Funds have since then been made available for more one-stop-shops and for enhancing the services of existing ones. While the department has been reluctant to take on full responsibility for funding these projects, it acknowledges that some capital costs need the help of funding from the central government to make the projects feasible. Building and land costs in particular have grown significantly in recent years.

To date, the government has spent a total of €30.5 million on one-stop-shop projects. In 2001, almost €11 million was made available. However, in 2002, the funding for one-stop-shop projects was reduced and only €8 million was available. This is due to the general tightening of public finances.

The scale of ambition regarding integrated service delivery varies considerably between local authorities, as does the amount of progress made to date. Ambitious local authorities, such as Donegal County Council, are striving towards integrated processing of requests and applications by engaging with different departments and agencies on behalf of individual clients. In other words, a holistic and personalised approach is taken to meeting people's service needs. Typically, the services provided in integrated service centres include those of the Revenue Commissioners, the Department of Social and Family Affairs and the local health board, but again there is considerable variation.

For example, in Donegal, integrated services centres (ISCs) are being established in each of the six electoral areas in the country to enable the customer to access information, advice and services across multiple channels and multiple agencies at a single point. It is based on the framework of the Public Services Broker (PSB), which aims to provide a single point of 'e-access' to all public services, irrespective of the delivering agency, level of government or geographical location.

Using the 'start small, think big, scale fast approach' the first integrated service centre has been set up in Carndonagh and remaining centres are due to be completed in the next couple of years. The idea is to start with a small number of services provided by the participating state agencies and Donegal Citizens Information Service, and Money Advice and Budgeting Service. As agencies re-engineer and reorganise, more services will be rolled out with further linkages to a number of agencies (Revenue, Departments of Education and Agriculture, Teagasc, Údarás, Comhairle) already identified. The Donegal ISCs provide a testbed to research and develop the multi-agency service delivery models required to enable the PSB framework to deliver integrated, multi-agency citizen services countrywide.

An important element of the new decentralised structures has been the strong corporate commitment from the senior management team in the council. The management team saw the possibilities of enhancing service delivery to the public with the help of integrated service centres in each electoral area (see Timonen, O'Donnell and Humphreys, 2003 for further details of this case study).

There are several reasons for the uneven development and progress of integrated service delivery across the county, but the interest and determination of local managers is perhaps the most decisive factor. It is essential that managers be committed, and show clear leadership. The only sanction or incentive that central government possesses is the granting or withholding of funding for the one-stop-shops. It appears, therefore, that local factors will continue to play the most important role in the future progress of integrated service delivery. It is possible, however, that the introduction of the Public Services Broker (PSB) will act as a catalyst for the development of integrated service delivery centres at the local level. The PSB will bring together packages of services required by citizens and make them available online. This concept would be complemented by local access centres, where trained advisers help customers to make use of the PSB technology that is designed to ease their interactions with the public services.

9.3 Key issues emerging and suggestions for future developments

While there are a number of excellent one-stop-shops, and some local authorities that are very committed to integrated service delivery, overall progress towards organising public service delivery in accordance with the one-stop-shop model has been limited. However, it is also clear that the re-organisation of service delivery around the one-stop-shop concept is a complex task and therefore requires long-term planning, commitment and funding, and co-operation between central and local government. When asked about integrated service delivery, several county and city managers noted that integration requires a significant commitment at central as well as local level to rationalise and integrate services.

There are significant differences between local authorities in terms of their geography and demographics, which also sets limits to the applicability of the one-stop-shop concept. Further, the differences between local authorities means that the one-stop-shop idea may not be suited to all of them. For instance, one-stop-shops may not be needed in some large urban areas that have well-established services within short distance of each other. However, disadvantaged urban areas such as parts of inner-city Dublin are likely to benefit from one-stop-shops that make services more accessible and bring them closer to service users/recipients. Decentralisation of service delivery may be the appropriate solution for most large counties, but not for smaller ones where distances to the main city or town are not great.

One of the main challenges of implementing one-stop-shop and integrated service delivery initiatives relates to difficulties in getting different service providers to co-operate, as evidenced by the comments by county and city managers who in general feel that much work remains to be done on the integration of service delivery with other service providers. A view was also expressed that co-location of service providers is not always or necessarily the answer to integrated service delivery. There is a need to develop a more pro-active approach to integrating services from other providers. Other significant problems noted by county and city managers include the dramatically increased building costs, unavailability of bandwidth and other technical prerequisites, internal management systems (including industrial relations issues), and the lack of adequate funding.

There may also be scope to develop the one-stop-shop concept further by linking it to enhancing local democracy. For instance, local councillors could have a role in monitoring and assessing the quality and availability of services in their area.

Some lessons can be learned from international experience. One-stop-shop projects have been initiated in a number of countries worldwide. There is considerable variation between countries in the approach that they have adopted. One-stop-shop-type initiatives are often aimed at improving access to both ICTs and public services. In a number of countries (e.g. Canada and Australia) the problem of 'e-exclusion' has been tackled by combining online e-government with other, more traditional channels of service delivery. In practice, this means that services are accessible electronically for those who want to use e-government services, but also over the phone, or in person, for those who are not comfortable with or cannot use e-government services.

For instance, the TIGERS (Trials of Innovative Electronic Regional Services) project in Tasmania involves experimenting with the delivery of integrated services across federal, state and local governments over the counter, over the phone and over the Internet. The services are made available at Service Tasmania shops and these include claims lodgement, information provision, appointment booking for services such as Centrelink, the Australian Taxation Office (ATO) and health and aged care. During a trial period of six months in 2001, rural clients of Centrelink, ATO and the Department of Veterans Affairs could attend interviews using videoconferencing facilities in three rural Service Tasmania shops.

In Portugal, www.lojadocidadao.pt is a long-established government portal, which provides links to a service for obtaining registration certificates and to a citizens information site. A large-scale experiment in comprehensive one-stop-shops has accompanied this portal. One-stop-shops are not about creating another public utility, but rather about decentralisation and rationalisation of service delivery. Around thirty public service providers operate through these one-stop-shops. The locations of one-stop-shops have been carefully chosen according to criteria that include easy urban access, easy accessibility by public transport and availability of parking spaces. The centres are wheelchair accessible, equipped with audio-visual equipment and facilitate clients with children. All the offices in a one-stop-shop are linked to an Intranet, which facilitates communication as well as the distribution and sharing of documents and an electronic book of appointments. An electronic system is also in place to count the number of clients per day, the average waiting time and the average time of processing a query. The opening hours for the one-stop-shops are very long, thus enabling working people flexible access (8.30 a.m. to 8.00 p.m. Monday to

Friday and 9.30 a.m. to 3.00 p.m. Saturdays). Some of the services that are available in the one-stop-shops are water, electricity, gas and telephone utilities; car registration; driving licence applications; passport applications; social security and health services (for more details on these and other examples see Timonen, O'Donnell and Humphreys, 2003).

Finally, it has been suggested that the role of local government may be undermined by e-government portals that provide a more centralised service provision (Lapre and Arjan, 2001). However, developments such as the Irish Public Services Broker will not substitute and are not designed to substitute for the physical presence of service delivery units at the local level; access to actual offices will always be needed. Because of this interdependence between the Public Services Broker and local service delivery units such as integrated service centres, it is of great importance that the links between central and local government are reinforced and made more real through greater collaboration and co-ordination.

10

Information and Communication Technologies

10.1 Intention of the modernisation programme

Enhancing the use of information technology was one of the key reform areas identified in *Better Local Government* (BLG) (1996). According to the information and communication technology (ICT) vision policy statement for the local government sector, it is intended that the strategic use of ICTs will help to 'build a local government system which is seen as the first choice for the delivery of a wide range of local services to all citizens, and a strategic partner with central government in preparing for and implementing the Information Society in Ireland' (Local Government Computer Services Board, 2000).

The corporate plan of Carlow County Council sets out the aims to be achieved through investment in IT and are typical of local authorities generally, to:

- improve the quality of their services to citizens and businesses
- improve decision making
- enhance the democratic role of elected members
- improve effectiveness of communication with all stakeholders
- get better value for money
- develop more effective partnerships with external organisations and agencies.

Effective use of ICTs should therefore enable seamless exchange of information between the central state, the local authorities and all other relevant institutions, as well as supporting strategic decision making and effective service delivery. It is intended that ICTs improve the working environment of staff within the local government sector, and minimise the impact of geographical constraints on service delivery. ICTs also have the potential to enhance citizens' participation in decision making (e.g. in the area of planning) through providing the public with up-to-date information in an easily understandable fashion and through enabling citizens to be consulted on policy issues (Local Government Computer Services Board, 2000).

10.2 The practice

Some local authorities have been very active in developing their information systems, including provision of infrastructure, systems implementation and staff training. A number of local authorities have expressed the intention to provide corporate networks connecting different offices and authorities such as town, library and area offices. Many local authorities are also developing Intranets for more effective internal communication and information sharing, and Extranets for instance for councillors. A number of county councils are also developing their fibre optic networks (broadband). There are still relatively few web-based applications that would enable citizens to deal electronically with local authorities, although for instance Kerry County Council can receive planning applications electronically. However, local authorities have developed and improved their Internet sites, and some of these enable users to send messages through e-mail links.

Wide area networking and communications infrastructures are in place and cover all parts of the local government system in Ireland, at least at a basic level, that enables communication between central and remote council offices. However, this technical capacity does not necessarily mean that work processes or service delivery are fully co-ordinated and integrated. The effective use of ICTs involves complex organisational changes that do not automatically follow the introduction of technology into local authorities; maximising the usefulness of ICTs still calls for a lot of work. However, it is interesting that not all county and city managers surveyed regard significant organisational change as necessary to get the most out of e-government initiatives. Roughly one third see a need for a significant amount of change, one third a need for a fair amount of change, and one-third a need for little or no organisational change.

Arguably, the most successful local authorities have been those that have applied the 'think big, start small, move fast' approach in their ICT strategies. In Meath, for example, in order to implement the decentralisation of services facilitated by ICT development, it was seen as necessary to overhaul fundamentally the existing organisational structure of the council (see Timonen, O'Donnell and Humphreys, 2003 for details)

Across the country, accessibility to the Internet and e-government services has been improved through a large-scale programme of installing PCs with Internet access in public libraries. In addition to Internet access, libraries also provide assistance to people wishing to familiarise themselves with the new technology. There are some 1400 PCs in the library network in Ireland. However, some capacity problems are emerging because this initiative has been so successful.

The various areas where the Local Government Computer Services Board (LGCSB) and local authorities have been working to plan and implement e-government include planning, housing, financial systems, electoral registers and higher education. The LGCSB is working together with Centre for Management and Organisation Development in the Department of Finance (CMOD) in areas such as the acquisition of XML tools to ensure that both central and local government use the same toolsets for workflow management etc. LGCSB is also working closely with CMOD, DELG and Reach for instance in creating and maintaining forms (the intention is that in future agencies and local authorities can put up and remove forms themselves without Reach having to do that). LGCSB has made its systems component based so that they can be combined with life-event based systems.

A generic Intranet for the local government system has been identified as a fundamental component of development in the Government Action Plan on the Information Society and in the DELG Strategic IT Plan. The local authorities' Intranet project enables local authorities to bring together all types of documents and make them centrally available across the organisation. As a result, the generic Intranet will provide a tool for better and faster service delivery by local authorities, and enable seamless communication between them. It has been proposed that the system would utilise the transportable elements of Meath County Council's Intranet to develop the generic system further (LGCSB, 2000). The Intranet will include among other things contact management systems that are mechanisms for integrating e-forms, letters and telephone contact information. This Intranet is to cover most local authorities (by autumn 2002, the generic Intranet had been rolled out to twenty-one local authority sites). The initial roll-out comprises a searchable phone book, a travel system for the electronic submission and assessment of travel expenses, an annual leave system, and immediate information on current events (road blockages, deadlines etc). In future, the Intranet will also include a content management system called eDirect. This will act as a frontline tracking system for communications between local authorities and citizens. The eDirect system will facilitate many of the objectives of the customer service action plans of local authorities, such as citizen response time, freedom of information and accurate communication on local issues. Citizens will be able to present queries as letters, e-mails, faxes, phone calls or front desk communications. The system then routes the message to the correct department, the answer is collated and checked, and returned to the citizen.

Many local authorities have already developed their own Intranets. Intranets tend to be most useful and functional when different sections within the local authority take responsibility for updating their information. Intranets typically contain staff phone lists, information on meetings, circulars and legislation, but they can also be used to record and track manager's orders, planning applications, motor taxation and HR issues. They enable improved communication and collaboration, faster and more efficient information retrieval, as well as lower operational costs and increased productivity (Keenan, 2002).

New financial management systems are being

implemented in all local authorities (see Chapter 6 for details). In the area of e-procurement (CMOD has primary responsibility here but LGCSB has also been involved) Kerry and Cork in particular have moved to advertising only on the web. When the VPN (virtual private network) comes out, LGCSB will have a role in it. In the area of housing, DELG is funding a 3-year housing project with LGCSB; one part of this will be an interactive browser-based enquiry system that enables citizens to check which services they are eligible for. Regarding electronic voter registration, issues of data protection have slowed down progress, but it will soon be possible to check whether one is on the register and if not, to apply online for registration. In the area of motor taxation, DELG is due to launch a pilot project that will enable online payment of tax.

In general, there is a lot happening in local authorities with regard to the implementation and use of ICTs. The support and guidance of the Local Government Computer Services Board is welcome. However, there is also a recognition among the county and city managers surveyed that progress to date is still relatively modest in many areas, and that greater efforts are needed to fully utilise ICTs, in both customer service provision and local authority administration (see Table 10.1). In particular, managers expressed concern about the need to ensure e-inclusion for all citizens.

10.3 Key issues emerging and suggestions for future developments

ICTs are closely related to economic progress and social cohesion. Ensuring economic and social progress involves ensuring that ICTs are available and actively used in all parts of the country, both by the private and public sectors, and by people of all socio-economic strata. As the local government system has a presence throughout the country, it is ideally positioned to promote the use of ICTs by the population. In other words, 'local government has the potential to contribute in a very positive way to the development of the information society in Ireland' (Local Government Computer Services Board, 2000). LGCSB

Table 10.1 County and city managers' views of ICT developments

	Not at all	A little	A fair amount	A lot	Very much	Total
More of our services are now delivered electronically to the customer	3%	41%	24%	28%	3%	100%
Information and communication technologies are being actively used to capture strategic information in the course of the everyday work of the authority	0%	17%	48%	14%	21%	100%

wants to involve the county and city development board structures in ensuring e-inclusion. It is intended that directors of community and enterprise will have a coherent plan to make best use of their resources to raise awareness and the utilisation of technology across the digital divide.

Local government is in a good position to capture a lot of strategic information in the course of the everyday work of local authorities. Effective use of ICTs can enhance the ability of local authorities to collect data that can then play an important role in the national policy planning process (e.g. in relation to waste management, environmental issues, housing and so on).

It is difficult to achieve consistency in the area of ICTs and local e-government, because most responsibility lies within local authorities that can set their own priorities and have varying resources. The role of county and city managers is very important. Also, the role of the manager-head of IT is a significant determinant in how effective and fast implementation of ICT strategies occurs.

Local authorities interact with many important players at the local and national level, and this interaction can be further enabled and enhanced with the help of ICTs. The main strength of local authorities and local service delivery agencies is that they are well placed for communicating with citizens, for receiving feedback and for delivering services in a genuinely interactive manner. The potential for local politicians and service delivery staff to influence policy can also be enhanced by creative use of ICTs to enable virtual organisations where people can have roles both at the central and local levels. E-government and more extensive use of ICTs may mean that the boundary between the local and the central will become more blurred.

Technology can be used to make people more aware of the issues that concern them. For instance, ICTs can be used to enhance local democracy and give people a greater say in how money is spent in their local communities. The ICT Vision for Local Government proposes greater involvement of citizens (e-democracy) in the spatial planning process: geographic information systems (GIS) that are already in use in many local authorities can be used to give citizens access to real-time information on spatial planning issues. Ultimately, as much as possible of the planning process should be visible on the Internet, so that for instance development plans will be put on the web, possibly containing intelligent maps that can provide 3D projections of planned developments, showing the impact on the street/landscape etc. Eventually, it may even be possible to register to receive notification of any planning applications that have been lodged/accepted near one's home. In general, more use could be made of council Internet sites.

ICTs may also enable local authorities to offer different services than those they have traditionally been providing. For instance, it is possible that direct access will be offered to information on laboratory results (e.g. on water quality), accident data (safer journeys for people), or that citizens will be able to notify areas with litter, traffic lights that do not work etc. In this way, ICTs can help to bring about greater closeness between citizens and local authorities.

PART 5

Conclusions and Recommendations

11

Conclusions and Recommendations

11.1 Introduction

The local government modernisation programme has set an ambitious agenda of change for the members, management and staff of local authorities. But is the modernisation programme working? What is working well, and where are the problems? Is the programme coherent? What are the main drivers of change? These are some of the questions addressed in this review of local government modernisation.

In summarising progress to date in implementing the modernisation programme, the three key outcomes of the programme identified in Chapter 1 – community leadership, efficiency and effectiveness, and quality services – are used to structure the findings. The programme was intended to enhance the community leadership role of local authorities; to improve the efficiency and effectiveness of the way authorities run their business; and to secure better quality services for local authority clients and customers and for local citizens more generally. What evidence is there of change in these areas? The findings for each are summarised in turn. This is followed by a general overview of progress to date and an outline of significant issues to be addressed in the future.

11.2 Community leadership

Two of the main aims of the local government modernisation programme are to develop political decision making and to widen the role of local government. The intention is to enhance the policy role of elected members – rebalancing the relationship with the administration – and to give local government a more prominent role in local development. These twin aims focus on developing the community leadership role of local government at the local level.

11.2.1 Developing political decision-making: main findings

Strategic policy committees (SPCs) have been established in all county and city councils. The purpose of these committees is to strengthen the policy-making role of elected councillors and to broaden participation in local government through the direct involvement of sectoral interests. The impact and effectiveness of SPCs varies significantly across and within authorities, as does the level of participation. While some SPCs are working well, there is a perceived danger of many SPCs turning into talking shops with little relevance to the actual work of local authorities. Two issues in particular are crucial to the future effectiveness of SPCs: the range and supply of policy issues and the level of participation and engagement of elected members and sectoral interests. The study identifies a number of critical factors which will determine the future success or otherwise of SPCs:

- The role of the chair of the SPC. The chair has a vital role in setting the tone for the operation of the SPC. Chairpersons should engage with the substantive content issues, facilitate interaction between councillors and the sectoral representatives, and establish links with the full council.
- The supply of meaningful policy issues. Here, the role of council staff in ensuring relevant papers/background material is crucial. The development of research capability within the local authority to enable policy issues to be explored is an important factor here.
- The engagement of councillors. The frequency and timing of meetings can be important, given the large number of meetings attended. So too is ensuring that councillors can see the linkage between policy discussions and the delivery of services to their constituents.
- The engagement and legitimacy of sectoral representatives. Ensuring that the appointment of sectoral representatives is as representative as practicable and that there is regular feedback between the sector and the representative enhances the legitimacy of the role.

Educating representatives on the role and workings of local government is also an important factor.

Area committees have been established or are in the process of being established in the majority of county and city councils. While not needed in all authorities, where they are in operation, they are generally seen as working very well. Area committees have enabled local issues and representations to be dealt with effectively at the local level, leaving more time at full council to address council-wide and corporate issues. Key factors in the longer-term success of area committees are the extent to which service provision is also decentralised and the effective interaction between area committees and area offices and officials.

The corporate policy group (CPG), which is intended to co-ordinate the work of the various SPCs, has only had a limited impact in many local authorities to date. Where the CPG is working well, it is acting as a useful sounding board to discuss contentious issues before they appear at full council. The CPG is also seen as enabling participating members to be better informed on policy issues. But in many councils the CPG is not seen as providing a forum giving direction to council priorities. Two main determinants in the success or otherwise of the CPG are the openness of managers and members to working together, and how effectively participating members feed back information to their own parties about the discussions at CPG meetings.

In general, the reforms are about enabling elected members to have more influence in shaping and directing policy. Area committees are widely seen as working well, whereas with regard to SPCs and the CPG the picture is more patchy. Further work is needed to secure an effective longer-term role for SPCs and the CPG in local authorities. In this context, a review of SPCs conducted for the DELG by the Institute of Public Administration in 2003 is intended to offer suggestions on ways forward.

11.2.2 Widening the role of local government: main findings

The establishment and operation of county and city

development boards (CDBs) has been the major feature in expanding the role of local government in local development and social inclusion. By the end of 2002, all county and city development boards had published their strategies for economic, social and cultural development. The operation of the CDBs has been greatly facilitated and enabled by the creation of the post of director of community and enterprise and associated support staff. Local government is now widely seen as having a stronger role in influencing and co-ordinating local development initiatives.

In moving forward, local authorities need to develop their research capacity and capability and to enhance their role in promoting good local governance. With regard to research capacity, there is a need to develop the evidence base for the implementation of social, economic and cultural strategies. This requires action both within local authorities and in terms of collaboration with other agencies, such as third-level institutions and the Local Government Management Services Board.

In terms of local governance, it needs to be recognised that the role of the local authority has moved beyond that of service provider. As one respondent in this study put it 'local government should be seen as the face of all government locally, not just delivering local government'. Local authorities need to establish themselves as leaders in the assessment of needs, policy direction and delivery of services to the community. As Stoker (2000) states: 'The big governance questions of this century will not be about which agency provides services but who decides the strategic direction for those services and how people can access them'. Local authorities, with their democratic mandate, are well placed to develop this strategic local governance role in terms of local development. The structural and process changes associated with the modernisation programme have put the necessary building blocks in place to develop collaborative arrangements to enhance local development. The next steps involve a move to shared decision making, shared resources and shared risk taking.

In all, there have been significant steps taken in

developing a new community leadership role for local government. The explicit addressing of the need to change the political/administrative interface is in contrast to reform in the civil service, where an evaluation of progress notes that management change had been the main aim, with little focus being put on the manner in which ministers and civil servants can most effectively interact in shaping policy (PA Consulting Group, 2002). While much remains to be done, the groundwork has been laid. In moving forward, it is important to note that the ultimate success of local community leadership development is not dependent on local authorities alone. Central government departments and their agencies must be given the direction to act in a way that facilitates rather than restricts the local leadership role of local authorities. Finally, it is worth re-emphasising the point that local community leadership by local authorities is not just about local authorities delivering their own services better. The focus is not so much on service provision as on local authorities establishing themselves as local leaders of publicly-funded services.

11.3 Efficiency and effectiveness

A significant part of the local government modernisation programme aims to ensure that the services run by local authorities are run efficiently and effectively. This encompasses planning for service provision and the use of resources, both human and financial.

11.3.1 Planning for service provision: main findings

Local authorities are at the early stages of engagement with corporate planning. Corporate plans are seen by management within authorities as a useful development, putting more focus on results and greater clarity and consensus on the main objectives to be achieved. But there is still work to do in terms of both improving the corporate planning process and in terms of securing widespread ownership of the plan among staff, and with the general public. Particular actions identified in this study to improve the planning process in the future include:

- Ensuring that the mission statement and mandate is clear and put into practice in terms of guiding the actions of the local authority. In reviewing the operating environment and conducting an environmental analysis, authorities should identify significant developments that will impact on the work of the authority in areas such as demographic change, new employment patterns, emerging social problems and issues, changing lifestyles and so on. Authorities should review public attitudes towards and needs for services as part of the environmental analysis. And they should ensure that objectives and strategies clearly flow from the analysis that is undertaken.
- Objectives and strategies should be more clearly defined and specified, and focused on outcomes where possible. Linking objectives and strategies to thematic issues emerging rather than simply organising by service programmes might be considered one way forward.
- Citizen/customer expectations and needs should be used to identify strategic issues to be addressed in the corporate plan, with clear linkage to the customer action plans as appropriate. It is to be expected that customer surveys, panels etc, referred to in the current plans, will be used as key sources of information regarding future developments.
- In further developing and shaping internal capacity, it will be important to match capacity to the strategic priorities identified, ensuring that the capacity exists to match the aspirations, and vice versa. In a similar light, with regard to resource allocation, plans and the planning process should reflect, in broad terms, the resources needed to achieve objectives and strategies.
- Regarding implementation and monitoring, there is a need to develop further the operational plans and performance indicators being used to assess progress. Practice in the selection and application of indicators should be reviewed so that information needed to manage more effectively is provided.

In particular, in terms of driving the planning process forward on a continuing basis, it is important that operational plans and annual reports are used effectively.

11.3.2 Managing financial resources: main findings

Much effort has gone into introducing a new financial management system (FMS) into local authorities. Significant progress has been made in getting the new FMS up and running. The process used to implement the financial changes has worked well. However, this process has been a lot more resource-intensive and the system less user-friendly than was initially envisaged. But compared to the introduction of new financial systems in the civil service, progress has been good. There is a significant degree of senior management engagement with the FMS. The re-vamping and upgrading of the finance function within local authorities has also occurred, with the creation of head of finance posts complemented by the creation of a financial/management accountant post.

The basic building blocks on which to develop improved financial management practice are now in place. But the main challenges and potential benefits associated with the implementation of the FMS now lie ahead. By and large, the active use of improved financial information in management decision making and performance improvement initiatives is yet to happen.

One significant challenge to address is the management of the cultural change involved for many managers and staff in moving to more active budgeting. Designating budget holders, and getting them to manage their budgets in a pro-active manner will require significant development of capacity and capability in this area.

Similarly, a further challenge is the introduction of more effective decisions on costing of service provision and assessment of the alternative approaches to service delivery. The basic financial data now being generated should be used to help in the exploration of alternative delivery mechanisms, including outsourcing, and in the benchmarking of performance of functions. It is important that progress made to date is seen as the first step on the way to a more integrated system of service and financial planning and management.

11.3.3 Managing human resources: main findings

Human resource management (HRM) was identified as a critical area for reform in the local government modernisation programme. In particular, the introduction of a new management structure with responsibility and accountability for developing strategic thinking was identified as a vital element in supporting the overall reform initiatives.

Some delays were experienced in introducing the new staffing structure, due to industrial relations difficulties and consequent union/management negotiations. By 2002, however, the new management tier of directors of service was in place, and consequent changes in staffing at middle management and other levels either in place or in the process of being introduced. One notable feature is that local authorities are structuring service and reporting arrangements to directors of service in different ways. It is important that steps are taken to learn from this diverse experience. While one model for all is inappropriate, it could be helpful if good practice and problems associated with different arrangements are identified and lessons learned from this experience. This is an issue that should be followed up by the Local Government Management Services Board.

More generally with regard to HRM reform, a number of issues emerge as needing attention in the future:

- Strategies in relation to the implementation of the HRM agenda should be detailed in the next iteration of corporate plans.
- There is a need for further development of management skills and competencies, particularly in the case of middle management and newly promoted staff.
- Outdoor staff need to be more integrated into the change programme.
- As a sector, local government is grappling with the issue of devolution of autonomy to authorities on HR issues,

and from HR units to line managers. There is a need to both further develop the strategic HR role of HR units, and to increase the role of line managers in the active management of HR issues within their spheres of responsibility.

- The development of a system of performance management and the implementation of training and development programmes are important requirements in assisting local authorities to overcome some of the challenges arising from the new staffing structures and the professionalisation of HR.

In terms of HR developments, it is also important to note the implementation of partnership arrangements in local authorities. Partnership has led to improved consultation and enhanced opportunities for staff to participate in decision making in many authorities. In moving forward, if partnership is to develop further it is important to set clear goals for the process and to engage with some of the harder edged HR/management issues.

In general, as with financial management reform, the HR changes arising from the modernisation programme can be characterised as at their early stages of development as yet. The new structures are in place, with the degree to which they are operating varying from authority to authority. The main challenge now is to operate the new structures so as to deliver services more effectively and efficiently. This will involve cultural change on the part of management and staff and action to ensure that the different elements of HR reform work effectively together.

Looking at the issue of efficiency and effectiveness in the round, the main point that emerges is that the foundations have been laid in the areas of planning, financial and human resource management to enable a more efficient and effective service to be provided by local authorities. The extent to which this happens in practice will be determined by the next stage of reform: building on these foundations to effect change in the planning and provision of services.

11.4 Delivering and securing quality services

This strand of the modernisation programme focuses on identifying and better servicing the needs of customers, clients and citizens. Achieving significant improvements in the quality of services delivered is a key objective of public service modernisation generally, including local government. At local government level, central to this drive for better quality services has been the development of customer action plans, service indicators, more integrated service delivery including one-stop-shops, and the use of information and communication technologies to support and underpin service initiatives.

11.4.1 Customer action plan and service indicators: main findings

Local authorities are required to produce and publish customer action plans (CAPs). These CAPs aim to (a) set out the actions authorities will take to achieve improvements in the quality of public services they are responsible for and (b) indicate how full effect will be given to the guiding principles for the delivery of quality customer service, as agreed across the public service. With regard to service indicators, local authorities are required as part of the modernisation programme to develop and use performance indicators to measure progress in relation to service standards.

The promotion and adoption of customer action plans by local authorities across Ireland in recent years has provided a valuable, introductory planning framework within which quality service issues can be successfully tackled. In areas such as improved information provision, the specification of service standards and indicators and commitment to introduce/improve complaint/appeal handling systems, this opportunity for planned improvement is being grasped by a number of local authorities across the county. Further efforts, however, are needed in many of the local authorities to drive forward quality improvements in line with the nationally agreed guiding principles for quality customer service.

Likewise, while some plans clearly demonstrate that

they have been produced via a process of effective internal and external stakeholder consultation, such plans are in a minority. Engagement with the public on quality service issues is one of the fundamental drivers of change from a customer perspective. There is a need for more widespread adoption of practices such as surveys of the customer base and the use of innovative consultation mechanisms. Systematic follow-on procedures should be developed to ensure that such survey and consultation exercises are acted on.

Similarly, while it is evident that some authorities have taken considerable care in both the preparation and presentation of their CAPs, with a demonstrated commitment to delivery, evaluation and substantive change, other plans are skeletal in content and superficial in their approach. Improved usage of central level guidance and support, combined with healthy inter-authority competition, co-operation and peer review, should help in improving both the quality and content of the next generation of CAPs as a whole.

In some plans, there is evidence that local authorities are engaging seriously with the significant challenges that arise when seeking to use CAPs as part of a wider strategy to mainstream customer service value more effectively. This can pose searching questions for existing management and work practices. Indeed, the whole-hearted adoption of customer service values often requires a fundamental reorientation of that organisation and a radical change in its prevailing culture. In this regard, engagement with external quality frameworks, such as the EU-wide Common Assessment Framework (CAF), can provide a valuable diagnostic tool, help promote joined-up quality-focused thinking in the organisation, as well as providing the opportunity for constructive benchmarking.

The development of service indicators is at an early stage and it is likely to be some time before it is possible to assess their contribution to improving the quality of service provided. At this stage, however, it could be useful to review experience to date and assess the degree to which the service indicators are being found useful in practice, or if the indicator set should be developed or changed in the light of experience. Certainly there is scope for more use to be made of comparative benchmarking of performance by authorities, either over time, against standards or with selected groupings of other authorities. It could also be useful in building on the service indicators experience to more actively engage with local citizens in the development and use of such indicators.

11.4.2 Integrated service delivery and one-stop-shops: main findings

The delivery of more integrated services at local level, with one-stop-shops as a main delivery mechanism for such integration, is a main component of the move to enhance the quality of service delivery. The intention is that instead of services being organised around bureaucratic structures, they are designed and delivered according to the needs of service users. In practice, the scale of ambition regarding integrated service delivery varies considerably between local authorities, as does the amount of progress made to date. The more ambitious authorities are striving towards integrating processing of requests and applications by engaging with different departments and agencies on behalf of individual clients.

While the integration of service delivery is often associated with the decentralisation of services, this is not necessarily the case in all circumstances. For smaller counties decentralisation may not be appropriate. However, where it occurs the re-organisation of service delivery on an integrated basis, in accordance with the principles of the one-stop-shop concept, is a complex task. The completion of this task requires long-term planning, top management commitment, and co-operation between central and local government. With regard to this latter point, the future development of the Public Services Broker concept has major implications. Because of the inter-dependence between the Public Services Broker and local service delivery units such as integrated service centres, it will be critical to future developments that the links between central and local government are reinforced and made more real through collaboration and co-ordination.

One of the main challenges of implementing more effective integration of service delivery relates to difficulties in getting different service providers to co-operate. Co-location of services is not necessarily the only or the right solution; more fundamental is the need to change practices so that service providers integrate and co-ordinate their services in a manner which suits the needs of the service recipient.

11.4.3 Using information and communication technologies: main findings

Increasing the use of information and communication technologies (ICTs) is one of the main areas of reform for local government. The aim is to improve the quality of service delivery and decision-making processes. Some local authorities have been very active in developing their information systems. Many have developed Intranets and Extranets and have developed and improved their Internet sites. There are though still relatively few web-based applications that enable citizens to deal electronically with local authorities. Managers are also very concerned about the need to ensure e-inclusion for all citizens.

The building up of technical capacity on its own, however, does not necessarily mean that work processes or service delivery are fully co-ordinated and integrated. The effective use of ICTs involves complex organisational changes that do not automatically follow the insertion of the technology into local authorities. This view is not necessarily shared by all managers within local authorities at present, and more work is needed to develop a shared understanding of the organisational changes needed to facilitate achievement of the full benefits of ICTs. The most successful authorities in terms of the application of ICTs appear to be those that have applied the 'think big, start small, move fast' approach in their ICT strategies.

With regard to future developments, e-government and more extensive use of ICTs may, when accompanied by organisational change, mean that the boundary between central and local government will become more blurred.

The management of this blurred interface will be a significant challenge. Also, ICTs can be used to enhance local democracy and to give people a greater say in how money is spent in their local communities. ICTs may also enable local authorities to offer different services than those they have traditionally been providing, bringing about greater closeness between citizens and local authorities.

Looking at the issue of delivering and securing quality services in total, a significant amount of progress has been made. Customer action plans, integrated service delivery practices and the use of ICTs are leading to more responsive service practices. But as with the other strands of modernisation, progress has been patchy and there is still a considerable amount of work to do. In terms of moving the quality agenda forward, local authorities must ensure that the component elements of the quality initiative – such as customer action plans, service indicators, one-stop-shops and the like – continue to be pursued with vigour and in a manner that puts the need of the service user first.

11.5 Local government modernisation

Looking at the actions that have been taken, it can be seen that significant progress has been made in implementing the local government modernisation programme. This assessment is backed up by the opinion of the Quality Assurance Group (QAG) for the local government sector established under the Programme for Prosperity and Fairness. The aim of the QAG was to monitor and report on progress on modernisation in the local government sector under a set of agreed indicators. The QAG was satisfied, based on reports from each local authority and a random examination of fourteen authorities, that considerable progress had been made in the implementation of the modernisation programme (Quality Assurance Group in the Local Government Sector, 2002).

But the steps taken to date should be seen as the first steps needed to create a vibrant local government service in Ireland. The foundations for progress have now been laid in areas such as financial management, human resource management, service quality and corporate planning. What is needed next is to consolidate and build on those foundations so as to deliver improved services to the public at local level. In moving forward, it is worth noting some of the main challenges to be faced, and identifying emerging management issues.

11.5.1 Challenges in moving forward

When asked about challenges to be addressed in rolling the modernisation programme forward, county and city managers were in no doubt that securing the necessary financial and other resources needed to see through implementation was the main challenge they saw. While recognising the limitations on public finances and the need to determine strategic priorities, there was seen to be a need for continuing support for the modernisation programme to secure full implementation.

The more active involvement of several key groups in moving the modernisation agenda forward has emerged from this study as a challenge. Many elected members, sectoral interest representatives on SPCs, and outdoor staff in local authorities, have only had limited engagement with the change process to date. There is a need for these groups to be more actively associated with change as things move forward.

The leadership and co-ordination role of local government in securing improved public services at local level – the local governance agenda – poses particular challenges. One of the main issues to be addressed here is ensuring buy-in to the leadership role of local authorities by central government departments and agencies. Departments and agencies other than the DELG need to be encouraged to work with and through local authorities on local policy and implementation issues they are engaged in.

Also, in this study a notable feature of change has been the diverse experience that exists across local authorities. Pockets of good practice exist in different authorities, with some moving forward faster than others in some areas. But local authorities are not particularly good at sharing and learning from this diverse experience in a structured way. More effort is needed to encourage and facilitate learning across local authorities. The supports given to directors of community and enterprise to network and collaborate offer a useful model here. Similarly the development of Intranets should facilitate information sharing.

Finally, there is the continuing challenge of ensuring appropriate supports to enable change. In this study, several examples of support structures which have been put in place and which have facilitated implementation of elements of the modernisation programme have been identified. This is the case particularly with regard to local government and local development, where the national task force, directors of community and enterprise and the Combat Poverty Agency anti-poverty learning network were noted as important structural supports in promoting modernisation.

11.5.2 Emerging management issues

In terms of management issues which are likely to receive a higher priority in coming years, a number of issues emerge from the discussions with key informants and the survey of county and city managers. These issues are either developments of existing issues or new issues emerging as concerns for managers:

- Performance management and measurement. Enhancing performance management practice at individual and team level and improving performance measurement systems are seen as significant priorities.
- The use of ICTs. Particularly with regard to the further development of integrated service delivery and the improvement of service provision to the general public and elected members, more use of ICTs and associated organisational changes are seen as major issues in the coming years.
- Training and development supports. Given the scale of change which has taken place, and which has still to occur, training and development supports for staff are crucial in terms of equipping them with the new skills and competencies needed.
- Regulatory reform. As the government's regulatory

reform agenda moves forward, the central role of local authorities both as enforcers of many regulations and as bodies subject to detailed regulation themselves will come under increased scrutiny.

- European governance. The European Commission's White Paper on European Governance (2001) proposes an enhanced role for local authorities in policy making at European level (Callanan, 2002)

11.6 Concluding comments

As *Better Local Government* (1996) notes: 'The local government system and the services it delivers play a crucial role in the economic and social life of the state'. Modernisation of local government management practices is important in promoting and continuing economic and social development.

A key point to emerge from this study is that the place of local government in public administration in Ireland is determined not only by the functions allocated to it or those services local government delivers directly. Equally important is the leadership role played by local government in the overall provision of local public services. To view local authorities as providers of a limited range of services is to miss the point. The potential for local government to influence and shape economic and social development locally is extremely significant. The degree to which this potential is translated into actual benefits will be determined by how local and central government continue to take forward the modernisation agenda.

References

Audit Commission (1999), *Planning to Succeed: Service and Financial Planning in Local Government*, London: Audit Commission

Allen, J. (2001), Presentation on social inclusion units to the Local Government Anti-Poverty Learning Network, Athlone 2001, run by the Combat Poverty Agency.

Asquith, A. and E. O'Halpin (1998), 'The changing roles of Irish local authority managers', *Administration*, Vol. 45, No. 4, pp. 76-92

Better Local Government – A Programme for Change (1996), Dublin: Department of the Environment

Bovaird, T. (2000), 'The role of competition and competitiveness in Best Value in England and Wales', Public Policy and Administration, Vol. 15, No. 4, pp. 82-99

Bovaird, T. and E. Löffler (2002), 'Moving from excellence models of local service delivery to benchmarking good local governance', *International Review of Administrative Sciences*, Vol. 68, No. 1, pp. 9-24

Boyle, R. (2000), *Performance Measurement in Local Government*, Committee for Public Management Research Discussion Paper No. 15, Dublin: Institute of Public Administration

Boyle, R. and S. Fleming (2000), *The Role of Strategy Statements*, Committee for Public Management Research Report No. 2, Dublin: Institute of Public Administration

Boyle, R. (2001), *A Review of Annual Progress Reports*, Committee for Public Management Research Discussion Paper No. 18, Dublin: Institute of Public Administration

Boyle, R. and P. C. Humphreys (2001), *A New Change Agenda for the Irish Public Service*, Committee for Public Management Research Discussion Paper No.17, Dublin: Institute of Public Administration

Boyle, R., L. Joyce, T. McNamara, M. Mulreany and A. O'Keefe (1996), 'Review of developments in the public sector in 1995', *Administration*, Vol. 43, No. 4, pp. 3-33

Boyle, R., T. McNamara, M. Mulreany and A. O'Keefe (1997), 'Review of developments in the public sector in 1996', *Administration*, Vol. 44, No. 4, pp. 3-41

Boyle, R., T. McNamara, M. Mulreany, A. O'Keefe and T. O'Sullivan (1998), 'Review of developments in the public sector in 1997', *Administration*, Vol. 45, No. 4, pp. 3-38

Boyle, R., T. McNamara, M. Mulreany, A. O'Keefe and T. O'Sullivan (1999), 'Review of developments in the public sector in 1998', *Administration*, Vol. 46, No. 4, pp. 3-40

Boyle, R., T. McNamara, M. Mulreany, A. O'Keefe and T. O'Sullivan (2000), 'Review of developments in the public sector in 1999', *Administration*, Vol. 47, No. 4, pp. 3-43

Boyle, R., T. McNamara, M. Mulreany, A. O'Keefe and T. O'Sullivan (2001), 'Review of developments in the public sector in 2000', *Administration*, Vol. 48, No. 4, pp. 3-42

Boyle, R., M. Callanan, J. Keogan, T. McNamara, M. Mulreany and T. O'Sullivan (2002), 'Review of developments in the public sector in 2001', *Administration*, Vol. 49, No. 4, pp. 7-49

Building an Inclusive Society (1998), Review of the National Anti-Poverty Strategy under the Programme for Prosperity and Fairness, Dublin: Department of Social, Community and Family Affairs

Burns, D., R. Hambleton and P. Hoggett (1994), *The Politics of Decentralisation*, London: the Macmillan Press Ltd.

Butler, P. (2002), *Evaluation of Customer Action Plans for the Public Service Modernisation Section*, Dublin: Department of the Taoiseach

Byrne, P. (2002), unpublished document prepared as background material for Nottingham Business School DBA programme, Dublin: Institute of Public Administration

Callanan, M. (2002), 'The white paper on governance: the challenge for central and local government', *Administration*, Vol. 50, No. 1, pp. 66-85

Callanan, M. (2003a), 'The role of local government', in M. Callanan and J. Keogan (eds.), *Local Government in Ireland,* Dublin: Institute of Public Administration

Callanan, M. (2003b), 'Assessing developments in local government', in M. Callanan and J. Keogan (eds.), *Local Government in Ireland*, Dublin: Institute of Public Administration

Collins, N. (1987), *Local Government Managers at Work*, Dublin: Institute of Public Administration

Community Workers Co-operative (2001), *Local Social Partnership Analysis*, Dublin: Community Workers Co-operative

Community Workers Co-operative (2002), *Local Social Partnership and the Community Sector – Are We Included?*, Dublin: Community Workers Co-operative

Chubb, B. (1983), *A Source Book of Irish Government*, Dublin: Institute of Public Administration

Davis, T. (2003), 'Local government finance: the financial process', in M. Callanan and J. Keogan (eds.), *Local*

Government in Ireland, Dublin: Institute of Public Administration

Department of the Environment and Local Government (1997), *Better Local Government: A Programme for Change – One Stop Shop Centres,* mimeo, Dublin: Department of the Environment and Local Government

Department of the Environment and Local Government (1998), *Report of the Task Force on Integration of Local Government and Local Development Systems*, Dublin: Department of the Environment and Local Government

Department of the Environment and Local Government (1999), *Strategic Policy Committees: Guidelines for Establishment and Operation*, Dublin: Department of the Environment and Local Government

Department of the Environment and Local Government (2000), *Service Indicators in Local Authorities*, Dublin: Department of the Environment and Local Government

Department of the Taoiseach and Equality Authority (2001), *Support Pack on the Equality/Diversity Aspects of Quality Customer Service for the Civil and Public Service*, Dublin: Department of the Taoiseach and Equality Authority

Dollard, G. (2003), 'Local government finance: trends in revenue and expenditure' in M. Callanan and J. Keogan (eds.), *Local Government in Ireland: Structures, Functions and Developments*, Dublin: Institute of Public Administration

Donegal County Council (2002), *Outline of Progress in the Implementation of Better Local Government*, Lifford: Donegal County Council

European Commission (2001), *European Governance: A White Paper,* Luxembourg: COM (2001) 428 Final

Fitzpatrick Associates (2002), *Review of the Local Government Anti-Poverty Learning Network: Initial Review*, Dublin: Combat Poverty Agency

Fitzpatrick Associates/ERM Ireland (2002), *Review of CDB Strategies*, Dublin: Department of the Environment and Local Government

Gaster, L. (1995), *Quality in Public Services*, Buckingham: Open University Press

Haslam, D. (2001), 'The county manager', in M. E. Daly (ed.), *County and Town – One Hundred Years of Local Government in Ireland: RTE Thomas Davis Lecture Series, Winter 1999*, Dublin: Institute of Public Administration

Ho, A. and P. Coates (2002), Case Study: *Citizens*

Identifying Performance Measures – The Experience of Iowa, paper written as part of Citizen Driven Government Performance Programme, Rutgers University, Newark, New Jersey.

Horan, A. (2001), 'Local authority financial management system: policy implications', presentation to City and County Engineers Conference, Great Southern Hotel, Killarney, 20 April.

Humphreys, P. (1998), *Improving Public Service Delivery*, Committee for Public Management Research Discussion Paper No. 7, Dublin: Institute of Public Administration

Humphreys, P. (2002), *Effective Consultation with the External Customer,* Committee for Public Management Research Discussion Paper No. 20, Dublin: Institute of Public Administration

Humphreys, P., S. Fleming and O. O'Donnell (1999), *Improving Public Services in Ireland: A Case-Study Approach*, Committee for Public Management Research Discussion Paper No. 11, Dublin: Institute of Public Administration

Institute of Public Administration (2002), *Training Needs Analysis*, Dublin: Local Government Management Services Board

Jaques, E. (1997), *Requisite Organization*, Arlington: Cason Hall & Co Publishers

Keenan, M. (2002), Content management in Kildare County Council, presentation given at InfoIreland conference, Dublin, September

Lapre, L. and V. Arjan (2001), 'Bridging the gap between citizen and administration', in D. Remenyi and F. Bannister (eds.), *Proceedings of the European Conference on E-Government*, Dublin, 27-28 September, pp. 247-259

Lazes, P. (2002), *Partnership in Local Authorities*, Dublin: Local Authority National Partnership Advisory Group

Limerick City Council Partnership Committee (2001), *Sharing the Same Goals,* Limerick: Limerick City Council

Local Government Computer Services Board (2000), *ICT Vision for Local Government,* Dublin: Local Government Computer Services Board

Modernising Government – The Challenge for Local Government (2000), Dublin: Department of the Environment and Local Government

Muintearas (2002), *A Place at the Table*, Leitir Moir: Muintearas

National Disability Authority (2002), *Ask Me: Guidelines for Effective Consultation with People with Disabilities*, Dublin: National Disability Authority

O'Riordan, J. and P. Humphreys (2003), *Developing an Effective Internal Customer Service Ethos*, Committee for Public Management Research Discussion Paper No. 24, Dublin: Institute of Public Administration

PA Consulting Group (2002a), *Evaluation of the Strategic Management Initiative*, Dublin: Department of the Taoiseach

PA Consulting Group (2002b), *Review of the Human Resource Function in Local Authorities*, Dublin: Local Government Management Services Board.

Partnership 2000 (1996), Dublin: Stationery Office

Pekdemir, U. (1995), 'New organisational forms within municipalities: the Tilburg model', paper tabled at a meeting of OECD public management service (PUMA) meeting, November, Paris

PricewaterhouseCoopers (2002), *Role Profiling and Training Needs Analysis*, Dublin: Local Government Management Services Board

Programme for Prosperity and Fairness (2000), Dublin: Stationery Office

Quality Assurance Group in the Local Government Sector (2002), *Summary Report from the Quality Assurance Group in the Local Government Sector*, unpublished report to the Department of the Taoiseach and Department of Finance

Quinlivan, A. (2001), 'The implementation of legislative changes in local government', paper presented at UCC conference, Department of Government, 28 September

Reeves, E. and M. Barrow (2000), 'The impact of contracting out on the costs of refuse collection services: the case of Ireland', *The Economic and Social Review*, Vol. 31, No. 2, pp. 129-150

Roche, D. (1982), 'Local government', *Administration*, Vol. 30, Nos 2 and 3, pp. 133-146

Sanderson I., J. Percy-Smith and L. Dawson (2001), 'The role of research in modern local government', *Local Government Studies*, Vol. 27, No. 8, pp. 59-78

Sheehy E. (2003), 'City and county management', in M. Callanan and J. Keogan (eds.), *Local Government in Ireland*, Dublin: Institute of Public Administration

Stoker, G. (2000), 'New beginning or end of an era?' *Public Finance,* June 23-29, pp. 16-18

Timonen, V., O. O'Donnell and P. Humphreys (2003), *E-*

Government and the Decentralisation of Service Delivery, Committee for Public Management Research Discussion Paper No.25, Dublin: Institute of Public Administration

Wilson, D. (2000), *'Towards local governance: rhetoric and reality'*, Public Policy and Administration, Vol. 15, No. 1, pp. 43-57

Zimmerman, J. F (1976), 'Role perceptions of Irish city and county councillors', *Administration*, Vol. 24, No. 4, pp. 482-500

APPENDIX 1

Key informant and local government interviews

Interviews and discussions were held with senior management from the following local authorities during the course of this study:

Donegal County Council
Dublin City Council
Galway City Council
Kerry County Council
Kildare County Council
Meath County Council
Sligo County Council
Waterford County Council
Westmeath County Council

In addition, interviews were conducted with managers in the following organisations that have a close linkage with local authorities:

ADM Ltd.
An Bord Pleanála
Combat Poverty Agency
Environmental Protection Agency
Housing Finance Agency
IMPACT
Local Government Unit, IPA
Local Government Computer Services Board
Local Government Management Services Board
National Building Agency
National Roads Authority
Office of the Ombudsman
SIPTU

APPENDIX 2

Questionnaire issued to county and city managers

ID. ☐☐

PRIVATE AND CONFIDENTIAL

QUESTIONNAIRE ON THE LOCAL GOVERNMENT MODERNISATION PROGRAMME

The Research Division of the Institute of Public Administration is undertaking a research study on behalf of the Committee for Public Management Research (CPMR) to examine the progress and impact to date of the local government modernisation programme. The intention is to identify and highlight good practice. The modernisation programme was initially set out in *Better Local Government* (1996) and elaborated on in *Modernising Government* (2000). The CPMR is composed of senior managers from a range of government departments, including the Department of the Environment and Local Government, along with representatives from TCD, UCD and the IPA.

As part of the study we would be grateful if you as county/city manager, could take the short time needed to complete the attached questionnaire. **All the information you provide will be treated in the strictest confidence by the IPA. Analysis will concentrate on broad trends, and individual authorities will not be identified in the findings of the survey.** The findings from the survey will provide one source of background information for the study. All county/city managers will receive a copy of the report, based on the study, on publication.

Questions require you to either circle the appropriate box or in the space provided give your own views and ideas.

Please contact Richard Boyle at (01) 2403756 (rboyle@ipa.ie) if you require any further information or assistance in filling out the questionnaire.

Please return the questionnaire to the IPA in the pre-paid envelope provided, by Friday 4 October 2002 at the latest.

Many thanks for your co-operation.

SECTION A: OVERVIEW

For each of the following two questions, please circle the most appropriate response.

	Not at all	A little	A fair amount	A lot	Very much
A1. The way the authority handles its work has improved over the past five years	1	2	3	4	5
A2. This change is mainly due to the local government modernisation programme	1	2	3	4	5

Would you like to comment on your answers to any of the questions raised above?

____

____

____

____

____

____

Do you have any other comments you would like to make about the impact of the local government modernisation programme in general?

____

____

____

____

____

____

____

____

____

____

SECTION B: ENHANCING DEMOCRACY

For each of the following four questions, please circle the most appropriate response.

	Not at all	**A little**	**A fair amount**	**A lot**	**Very much**
B1. Strategic Policy Committees are meaningfully engaged in the examination of local strategic policy issues	1	2	3	4	5
B2. Councillors and sectoral interest representatives are working well together on Strategic Policy Committees	1	2	3	4	5
B3. The Corporate Policy group is acting as a forum for giving direction to council priorities, discussing progress and informing members on key policy issues	1	2	3	4	5
ANSWER B4 ONLY IF YOU HAVE ESTABLISHED AREA COMMITTEES B4. Area committees have succeeded in freeing full council meetings to deal more with council-wide policy issues	1	2	3	4	5

Do you have any other comments or suggestions for improvements you would like to make about:

(a) Strategic Policy Committees

____

____

____

____

(b) The Corporate Policy Group

____

____

____

____

(c) Area Committees

____

____

SECTION C: LOCAL GOVERNMENT AND LOCAL DEVELOPMENT

For each of the following three questions, please circle the most appropriate response

	Not at all	A little	A fair amount	A lot	Very much
C1. Local government has a stronger role now in influencing and co-ordinating local development initiatives	1	2	3	4	5
C2. Social inclusion is a more prominent item on the local authority agenda than in the past	1	2	3	4	5
C3. The local authority is seen by the public as the leader of local development initiatives in the area	1	2	3	4	5

Would you like to comment on your answers to any of the questions raised above?

____

____

____

____

____

____

Do you have any other comments you would like to make about local government's role in co-ordinating local development?

____

____

____

____

____

____

____

SECTION D: PLANNING AND FINANCIAL MANAGEMENT

For each of the following four questions, please circle the most appropriate response.

	Not at all	A little	A fair amount	A lot	Very much
D1. The corporate plan usefully prioritises the council's main objectives and gives us more of a focus on results	1	2	3	4	5
D2. The corporate plan is widely understood and 'owned' by staff	1	2	3	4	5
D3. Operational plans have helped improve the performance of the authority	1	2	3	4	5
D4. The quality of financial information available within the authority has improved in recent years	1	2	3	4	5

Do you have any other comments or suggestions for improvement you would like to make about:

(a) The Corporate Plan

____

____

____

____

(b) Operational Plans

____

____

____

____

(c) The financial management system

____

____

____

____

SECTION E: HUMAN RESOURCE MANAGEMENT

For each of the following four questions, please circle the most appropriate response.

	Not at all	A little	A fair amount	A lot	Very much
E1. The introduction of a new management structure has resulted in a more strategic approach to the delivery of services within the authority	1	2	3	4	5
E2. The HR/personnel unit is more professional and strategic in its approach to HR issues	1	2	3	4	5
E3. Line managers are more involved in the active management of their staff	1	2	3	4	5
E4. Partnership has helped to develop/resolve initiatives that would not have been introduced/resolved otherwise	1	2	3	4	5

Would you like to comment on your answers to any of the questions raised above?

____

____

____

____

____

____

Do you have any other comments you would like to make about the human resource management changes arising from the local government modernisation programme?

____

____

____

SECTION F: SERVICE DELIVERY

For each of the following four questions, please circle the most appropriate response.

	Not at all	A little	A fair amount	A lot	Very much
F1. The Customer Action Plan has given a clearer focus to quality service delivery issues	1	2	3	4	5
F2. Service indicators are actively used to monitor our delivery of quality services	1	2	3	4	5
F3. Integration of service delivery with other service providers (FÁS, health boards etc) means customers are getting better services from government generally at the local level	1	2	3	4	5
ANSWER F4 ONLY IF YOU HAVE DECENTRALISED SERVICE DELIVERY TO AREA OFFICES F4. The local delivery of council services through decentralised offices is leading to a higher quality of service to the customer	1	2	3	4	5

Would you like to comment on your answers to any of the questions raised above?

____

____

____

____

____

____

Do you have any other comments you would like to make about service delivery changes arising from the modernisation programme?

____

____

____

SECTION G: INFORMATION AND COMMUNICATION TECHNOLOGIES

For each of the following three questions, please circle the most appropriate response.

	Not at all	A little	A fair amount	A lot	Very much
G1. More of our services are now delivered electronically to the customer	1	2	3	4	5
G2. To get the most out of e-government initiatives, changes in the organisational structure of the council are required	1	2	3	4	5
G3. Information and communication technologies are being actively used to capture strategic information in the course of the everyday work of the authority	1	2	3	4	5

Would you like to comment on your answers to any of the questions raised above?

____

____

____

____

____

____

Do you have any other comments you would like to make on the impact of ICTs on the way your authority works?

____

____

____

____

____

SECTION H: GENERAL

Do you have any additional comments about:

(a) Implementation of the local government modernisation programme

(b) Challenges to be addressed in rolling forward the modernisation programme

(c) Emerging management issues which you would like to see given a high priority in the coming years

Thank you for completing the questionnaire.

Please return in the pre-addressed envelope by Friday 4 October 2002

Appendix 3

Summary of tabulated responses to questionnaire issued to county and city managers

NOTE: Figures may not add up exactly to 100 per cent in all cases due to rounding.

Section A: Overview

	Not at all	A little	A fair amount	A lot	Very much	Total
A1 The way the authority handles its work has improved over the past five years	0	2	5	15	7	29
A2 This change is mainly due to the local government modernisation programme	0	4	12	11	2	29

%	Not at all	A little	A fair amount	A lot	Very much	Total
A1 The way the authority handles its work has improved over the past five years	0%	7%	17%	52%	24%	100%
A2 This change is mainly due to the local government modernisation programme	0%	14%	41%	38%	7%	100%

Section B: Enhancing Democracy

	Not at all	A little	A fair amount	A lot	Very much	Total
B1 Strategic policy committees are meaningfully engaged in the examination of local strategic policy issues	0	6	12	9	2	29
B2 Councillors and sectoral interest representatives are working well together on strategic policy committees	0	3	15	10	1	29
B3 The corporate policy group is acting as a forum for giving direction to council priorities, discussing progress and informing members on key policy issues	1	8	8	5	7	29
B4* Area committees have succeeded in freeing full council meetings to deal more with council-wide policy issues	1	1	5	4	9	20

%	Not at all	A little	A fair amount	A lot	Very much	Total
B1 Strategic policy committees are meaningfully engaged in the examination of local strategic policy issues	0%	21%	41%	31%	7%	100%
B2 Councillors and sectoral interest representatives are working well together on strategic policy committees	0%	10%	52%	35%	3%	100%
B3 The corporate policy group is acting as a forum for giving direction to council priorities, discussing progress and informing members on key policy issues	3%	28%	28%	17%	24%	100%
B4* Area committees have succeeded in freeing full council meetings to deal more with council-wide policy issues	5%	5%	25%	20%	45%	100%

* Does not apply to all local authorities

Section C: Local Government and Local Development

	Not at all	A little	A fair amount	A lot	Very much	Total
C1 Local government has a stronger role now in influencing and co-ordinating local development initiatives	0	1	6	14	8	29
C2 Social inclusion is a more prominent item on the local authority agenda than in the past	1	1	11	12	4	29
C3 The local authority is seen by the public as the leader of local development initiatives in the area	0	2	10	12	5	29

%	Not at all	A little	A fair amount	A lot	Very much	Total
C1 Local government has a stronger role now in influencing and co-ordinating local development initiatives	0%	3%	21%	48%	28%	100%
C2 Social inclusion is a more prominent item on the local authority agenda than in the past	3%	3%	38%	41%	14%	100%
C3 The local authority is seen by the public as the leader of local development initiatives in the area	0%	7%	35%	41%	17%	100%

Section D: Planning and Financial Management

	Not at all	A little	A fair amount	A lot	Very much	Total
D1 The corporate plan usefully prioritises the council's main objectives and gives us more of a focus on results	0	0	5	12	12	29
D2 The corporate plan is widely understood and 'owned' by staff	0	4	15	7	3	29
D3 Operational plans have helped improve the performance of the authority	0	1	11	15	1	28
D4 The quality of financial information available within the authority has improved in recent years	0	4	10	11	4	29

%	Not at all	A little	A fair amount	A lot	Very much	Total
D1 The corporate plan usefully prioritises the council's main objectives and gives us more of a focus on results	0%	0%	17%	41%	41%	100%
D2 The corporate plan is widely understood and 'owned' by staff	0%	14%	52%	24%	10%	100%
D3 Operational plans have helped improve the performance of the authority	0%	4%	39%	54%	4%	100%
D4 The quality of financial information available within the authority has improved in recent years	0%	14%	34%	38%	14%	100%

Section E: Human Resource Management

	Not at all	A little	A fair amount	A lot	Very much	Total
E1 The introduction of a new management structure has resulted in a more strategic approach to the delivery of services within the authority	0	2	8	14	5	29
E2 The HR/personnel unit is more professional and strategic in its approach to HR issues	0	4	14	10	1	29
E3 Line managers are more involved in the active management of their staff	0	3	15	9	2	29
E4 Partnership has helped to develop/resolve initiatives that would not have been introduced/resolved otherwise	0	7	14	4	4	29

%	Not at all	A little	A fair amount	A lot	Very much	Total
E1 The introduction of a new management structure has resulted in a more strategic approach to the delivery of services within the authority	0%	7%	28%	48%	17%	100%
E2 The HR/personnel unit is more professional and strategic in its approach to HR issues	0%	14%	48%	35%	3%	100%
E3 Line managers are more involved in the active management of their staff	0%	10%	52%	31%	7%	100%
E4 Partnership has helped to develop/resolve initiatives that would not have been introduced/resolved otherwise	0%	24%	48%	14%	14%	100%

Section F: Service Delivery

	Not at all	A little	A fair amount	A lot	Very much	Total
F1 The Customer Action Plan has given a clearer focus to quality service delivery issues	0	1	7	17	4	29
F2 Service indicators are actively used to monitor our delivery of quality services	0	6	13	7	3	29
F3 Integration of service delivery with other service providers (FÁS, health boards etc) means customers are getting better services from government generally at the local level	1	14	10	4	0	29
F4* The local delivery of council services through decentralised offices is leading to a higher quality of service to the customer	0	0	4	4	3	11

%	Not at all	A little	A fair amount	A lot	Very much	Total
F1 The Customer Action Plan has given a clearer focus to quality service delivery issues	0%	3%	24%	59%	14%	100%
F2 Service indicators are actively used to monitor our delivery of quality services	0%	21%	45%	24%	10%	100%
F3 Integration of service delivery with other service providers (FÁS, health board etc) means customers are getting better services from government generally at the local level	3%	48%	35%	14%	0%	100%
F4* The local delivery of council services through decentralised offices is leading to a higher quality of service to the customer	0%	0%	36%	36%	27%	100%

* Does not apply to all local authorities

Section G: Information and Communication Technologies

	Not at all	A little	A fair amount	A lot	Very much	Total
G1 More of our services are now delivered electronically to the customer	1	12	7	8	1	29
G2 To get the most out of e-government initiatives, changes in the organisational structure of the council are required	3	6	10	4	5	28
G3 Information and communication technologies are being actively used to capture strategic information in the course of the everyday work of the authority	0	5	14	4	6	29

%	Not at all	A little	A fair amount	A lot	Very much	Total
G1 More of our services are now delivered electronically to the customer	3%	41%	24%	28%	3%	100%
G2 To get the most out of e-government initiatives, changes in the organisational structure of the council are required	11%	21%	36%	14%	18%	100%
G3 Information and communication technologies are being actively used to capture strategic information in the course of the everyday work of the authority	0%	17%	48%	14%	21%	100%

Appendix 4

Article 28A of Bunreacht na hÉireann

1. The State recognises the role of local government in providing a forum for the democratic representation of local communities, in exercising and performing at local level powers and functions conferred by law and in promoting by its initiatives the interests of such communities.
2. There shall be such directly elected local authorities as may be determined by law and their powers and functions shall, subject to the provisions of this Constitution, be so determined and shall be exercised and performed in accordance with law.
3. Elections for members of such local authorities shall be held in accordance with law not later than the end of the fifth year after the year in which they were last held.
4. Every citizen who has the right to vote at an election for members of Dáil Éireann and such other persons as may be determined by law shall have the right to vote at an election for members of such of the local authorities referred to in section 2 of this Article as shall be determined by law.
5. Casual vacancies in the membership of local authorities, referred to in section 2 of this Article shall be filled in accordance with law.

APPENDIX 5

Guiding principles for the delivery of quality customer service

Quality standards: Publish a statement that outlines the nature and quality of service which customers can expect, and display it prominently at the point of service delivery.

Equality/diversity: Ensure the rights to equal treatment established by equality legislation, and accommodate diversity, so as to contribute to equality for the groups covered by the equality legislation (under the grounds of gender, marital status, family status, sexual orientation, religious belief, age, disability, race and membership of the Traveller Community). Identify and work to eliminate barriers to access to services for people experiencing poverty and social exclusion, and for those facing geographic barriers to services.

Physical access: Provide clean, accessible public offices, which ensure privacy, comply with occupational and safety standards and, as part of this, facilitate access for people with disabilities and others with specific needs.

Information: Take a pro-active approach in providing information that is clear, timely and accurate, is available at all points of contact and meets the requirements of people with specific needs. Ensure that the potential offered by Information Technology is fully availed of and that the information available on public service websites follows the guidelines on web publication. Continue to drive for simplification of rules, regulations, forms, information leaflets and procedures.

Timeliness and courtesy: Deliver quality services with courtesy, sensitivity and the minimum delay, fostering a climate of mutual respect between provider and customer. Give contact names in all communications to ensure ease of ongoing transactions.

Complaints: Maintain a well publicised, accessible, transparent and simple-to-use system of dealing with complaints about the quality of service provided.

Appeals: Similarly, maintain a formalised, well-publicised, accessible, transparent and simple-to-use system of appeal/review for customers who are dissatisfied with decisions in relation to services.

Consultation and evaluation: Provide a structured approach to meaningful consultation with, and participation by, the customer in relation to the development, delivery and review of services. Ensure meaningful evaluation of service delivery.

Choice: Provide choice, where feasible, in service delivery including payment methods, location of contact points, opening hours and delivery times. Use available and emerging technologies to ensure maximum access and choice, and quality of delivery.

Official languages equality: Provide quality services through Irish and/or bilingually and inform customers of their rights to choose to be dealt with through one or other of the official languages.

Better co-ordination: Foster a more co-ordinated and integrated approach to delivery of public services.

Internal customer: Ensure staff are recognised as internal customers and that they are properly supported and consulted with regard to service delivery issues.

Appendix 6

Local Authority Service Indicators

H: Housing

H.1 The percentage of dwellings that are empty:

a) Available for letting or awaiting minor repairs

b) Others

H.2 Average time taken to relet dwellings available for letting or awaiting minor repairs

R: Roads

R.1 Cost per square metre for surface dressing

R.2 Percentage of local roads surface dressed per annum

R.3 Percentage of regional roads surface dressed per annum

M: Motor Taxation

M.1 Percentage of applications which are postal

M.2 Average number of postal applications and percentage of overall postal applications which are dealt with (i.e. disc issued) from receipt of the application:

a) on the same day

b) on the third day or less

c) on the fifth day or less

d) over 5 days

M.3 Public opening hours: average number of hours per week

M.4 Transaction costs (direct) per unit

E: Environmental Services

E.1 Percentage of river channel which is:

a) unpolluted

b) slightly polluted

c) moderately polluted

d) seriously polluted

E.2 Percentage of drinking water samples in compliance with statutory requirements

E.3 Time, in minutes, to mobilise fire brigades in

a) full time stations

b) part time stations

E.4 Bring-Facilities

Category	Number of Facilities*	Number of locations per 5,000 of population
Glass		
Cans		
Textiles		
Batteries		
Oils		
Others		

*including facilities provided other than by the local authority

E.5 Litter

a) Number of litter wardens: full time; part time; and in total as a proportion of the population (e.g. 1:10,000)

b) Number of on-the-spot fines

c) Number of prosecutions

P: Planning

Category	No. of applications determined	% determined within 8 weeks	Average time taken to determine	% of grants	% of refusals	% appealed	Results of appeals: % which uphold the council's decision*	Results of appeals: % which reverse the council's decision
Individual Houses								
Housing Development								
Other: not requiring EIA								
Other: requiring EIA								

* with or without amendment

Rev: Revenue Collection

Rev.1 House Rent

a) Amount collected at year end as a percentage of amount due

b) Percentage of arrears:

(i) 1-3 weeks old

(ii) 4-6 weeks old

(iii) more than 6 weeks old

Rev.2 House Repayments

a) Amount collected at year end as a percentage of amount due

b) Percentage of arrears:

(i) 1 month old

(ii) 2-3 months old

(iii) more than 3 months

Rev.3 Rates – Amount collected at year end as a percentage of amount due

C: Corporate Health

C1 Percentage of working days lost to sickness absence

L: Library Services

L.1 Public opening hours - average number of hours per week in: towns of 5,000 people or more

L.2 Number of items issued per head of population (county/city wide) for:

a) books

b) other items

(Source: Department of the Environment and Local Government, 2000)

Research Report Series

1. *Partnership at the Organisation Level in the Public Service*, Richard Boyle, 1998
2. *The Role of Strategy Statements*, Richard Boyle and Síle Fleming, 2000
3. *Flexible Working in the Public Service*, Peter C. Humphreys, Síle Fleming, Orla O'Donnell, 2000
4. *A QCS Mark for the Irish Public Service*, Peter C. Humphreys, Michelle Butler, Orla O'Donnell, 2001